WALKS FOR ALL AGES
CARMARTHENSHIRE
SWANSEA & THE GOWER

iStock

WALKS FOR ALL AGES

CARMARTHENSHIRE SWANSEA & THE GOWER

HUGH TAYLOR & MOIRA McCROSSAN

BRADWELL
BOOKS

Published by Bradwell Books
9 Orgreave Close Sheffield S13 9NP
Email: books@bradwellbooks.co.uk

British Library Cataloguing in Publication Data: a catalogue record for this book is available from the British Library.

1st Edition

ISBN: 9781909914360

Print: Gomer Press, Llandysul, Ceredigion SA44 4JL

Design by: Erik Siewko Creative, Derbyshire.
eriksiewko@gmail.com

Photograph Credits: © Hugh Taylor & Moira McCrossan
and credited seperately where applicable.
Front Cover: iStock

Maps: Contain Ordnance Survey data
© Crown copyright and database right 2015

Ordnance Survey licence number 100039353

The information in this book has been produced in good faith and is intended as a general guide. Bradwell Books and its authors have made all reasonable efforts to ensure that the details are correct at the time of publication. Bradwell Books and the author cannot accept any responsibility for any changes that have taken place subsequent to the book being published. It is the responsibility of individuals undertaking any of the walks listed in this publication to exercise due care and consideration for the health and wellbeing of each other in the party. Particular care should be taken if you are inexperienced. The walks in this book are not especially strenuous but individuals taking part should ensure they are fit and able to complete the walk before setting off.

INTRODUCTION

THIS IS THE PART OF WALES THAT GAVE DYLAN THOMAS TO THE WORLD. USE THIS BOOK TO EXPLORE HIS 'UGLY LOVELY TOWN' OF SWANSEA, VISIT THE HOUSE IN WHICH HE WAS BORN AND BROUGHT UP AND THEN EXPLORE THE GREEN OASIS OF CYMDONKIN PARK WHERE HE PLAYED AS A BOY AND DEVELOPED HIS WONDERFUL IMAGINATION.

Then head for the country town of Llansteffan where he spent part of his childhood living on the farm of his aunt and uncle. From these visits came poems like ' Fern Hill' and 'In Memory of Anne Jones' written after his aunt died. She is buried in the nearby village of Llanybri close to the grave of another of Dylan's friends, the poet Lynette Roberts. Dylan had been the best man at her marriage to his friend Keidrych Rhys. Another of his literary pals, the novelist Glyn Jones, lies in Llansteffan churchyard.

Dylan Thomas and his wife are interred in the churchyard at Laugharne, the little town on the estuary where he spent the last years of his life living in a boathouse provided by a benefactor. It's now a museum and in the grounds is the wooden shed where he wrote his classic 'Under Milk Wood'. The walk there follows the route of his 3oth birthday walk to St John's Hill in 1944 after which he wrote ' Poem in October'.

In Margam Country Park keen fans of Torchwood and Doctor Who will experience a touch of Déjà vu and also come across a replica of the Tardis, his distinctive blue Police Box. Although it can't be used for Time Travel this book can guide you back into the ancient and often warlike past.

Neolithic Chambers testify to the earliest inhabitants while an artificial warren is evidence that it was the Romans who were responsible for unleashing the rabbit upon us when they introduced it as a source of meat.

They also took over earlier strategic locations including Iron Age Forts and constructed more advanced fortifications. Later the Normans and then the English would occupy the same sites. The Welsh were not happy to be subjugated and rebelled on several occasions, leaving stories and legends of daring heroes.

Owain Lawgoch, the last true Prince of Wales, supposedly rests with his army in a cave under Carred Cennen waiting the call to return and free his people. Owen Glyndŵr emerged during the 15th century War of Liberation to sack and burn. When the English King retaliated with a massive army Glyndŵr disappeared and was never captured or betrayed. But his follower Llywelyn ap Gruffudd Fychan of Landovery was tortured, hung, drawn and quartered for refusing to give up his leader. A female hero, Princess Gwenllian, valliently fought against the Norman invaders, was defeated and beheaded. Her barbaric death resulted in The Great Revolt when all of Wales rose up.

In more recent history the famous female aviator, Amy Johnson used Pendine sands as a runway for one of her record attempts and later the same beach was used for the World land Speed record attempts. John Godfrey Parry Thomas shattered the record on Pendine Sands on 29th April 1926 when he reached 171.02mph. The following March he was killed on the sands making another attempt. His car was buried in the sands but recovered, restored and is now in the nearby Museum of Speed.

We have had a wonderful time researching and selecting the walks for this book and we hope you enjoy them as much as we have.

LAUGHARNE

Take the walk that Dylan Thomas took on his 30th birthday, 27 October 1944, around the estuary and through some lovely woodlands, and then continue along part of the coastal path.

Dylan Thomas, who has been called the greatest poet writing in English in the 20th century, lived at Laugharne for the last few years of his life. But those years were among his most productive as an adult. It was here that he wrote his last and perhaps best-known work, Under Milk Wood. It is a play for voices, which brings to life an entire community, many of whom were recognisable Laugharne characters. He called Laugharne 'the strangest town in Wales'.

He lived in several houses in the town, but the last was the Boat House, which sits above the estuary of the River Tâf, overlooking the wide salt marshes and mud banks, with its wealth of bird life. He was fascinated by birds and they featured strongly in his poetry, including the poem he wrote about his Birthday Walk.

> *My birthday began with the water-*
> *Birds and birds of the of the winged trees flying my name*

And then in the woodlands:

> *A springful of larks in a rolling*
> *Cloud and the roadside bushes brimming with whistling*
> *Blackbirds and the sun of October*

He sees the turning of the season and is transported to his childhood.

> *And I saw in the turning so clearly a child's*
> *Forgotten mornings when he walked with his mother*

And he feels his own years and his mortality.

> *O may my heart's truth*
> *Still be sung*
> *On this high hill in a year's time.*

And indeed he was still there in a year's time — but he did not see his fortieth birthday.

For many years Bob Stevens has taken this walk every year on his birthday, which, like Dylan Thomas's, is in October. He took his children along and read them the poem. He was inspired to share the pleasure they have had by opening the walk to the public and sharing his knowledge of both the poem and the local area. Bob has designed boards with the poem printed on it and information about all the things that you can see.

If you really want to share Dylan Thomas's experience, you can download a recording of Thomas reading it and listen to his mellifluous tones as you walk.

THE BASICS

Distance: 3 miles / 4.8km
Gradient: One long steep descent mainly on stairs and one very steep ascent
Severity: Strenuous, but most strenuous part can be cut out if desired
Time: 2 hrs
Stiles: Five
Map: OS Explorer 177 (Carmarthen & Kidwelly)
Path description: Woodland paths (one narrow and rough), steps, field and road
Start point: Car park at Laugharne Castle (GR SN 301106)
Parking: Laugharne Castle car park (SA33 4SS)
Landscape: Estuary, salt marsh and woodland
Dog friendly: Yes, apart from stiles
Toilets: On the main street near the car park
Nearest food: There are several pubs and cafés in the town and a tearoom at Dylan's Boathouse

1. From the car park head along the tarmac path along the estuary, signposted Dylan's Birthday Walk. Continue through a gate and to a signpost pointing right. Cross a wooden bridge and head uphill on a woodland path.

2. Continue on this path through the woods with the estuary on your left, stopping at the information boards as you go. At some points the view of the estuary opens up and there are seats to sit and enjoy the view or the peace or the sounds of sea and woodland. Eventually you will come to a fork. Take the left fork, following a signpost to 'the Last Verse'.

3. This is the end of the Birthday Walk but you can continue from here down some steep steps to follow the coastal path. If you want to miss out the steep parts you can go back to the fork and follow the path through the woods, which will bring you out at the hamlet on the road at point 5. At the bottom of the steps go through a gate and the path continues on the level. The view opens up across the merse and you will go through a kissing gate. Eventually you arrive at Salt House Farm. There is a kissing gate to the left, which allows you to detour around the farm.

4. Continue ahead on a good level path until, at a bend, you will see a waymarker to the right. Turn up here, over a stile and bear left on a very steep, narrow path through woodland. You will emerge at a pair of stiles – one ahead and then another at right angles on the right. Cross both of them and go left following the path along the edge of the field and then over another stile and downhill to the road. Cross another stile and go right on the road.

5. Follow the road through a hamlet and eventually reach a lane to the right. Turn along here and then next left at a footpath sign. Go through a gate and follow the footpath

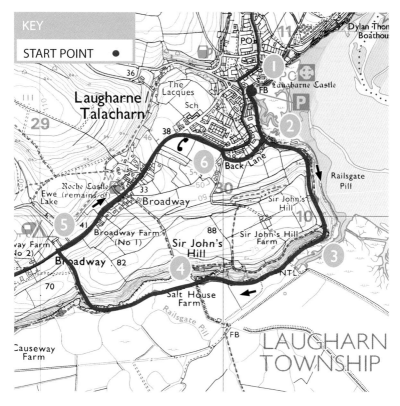

to the right of a house and through another gate, to reach a shady woodland path, which may be muddy, heading downhill.

6. This path emerges on the path along the estuary. Turn left and retrace your steps to the car park.

PENDINE

A BEACH WALK WITH A DIFFERENCE. FOLLOW IN THE TYRE TRACKS OF SOME OF THE LEGENDS OF FLIGHT AND MOTOR RACING ALONG PENDINE SANDS, THEN TRY YOUR HAND AT BEACHCOMBER ART.

On 22 July 1933, Amy Johnson, the first female to fly solo from Britain to Australia, and her husband Jim Mollison took off from here in their twin-engined de Havilland 84 Dragon Moth. Short of fuel, they crash-landed just short of their goal but escaped serious injury and were welcomed back as heroes.

John Godfrey Parry Thomas will forever be associated in Welsh minds with Pendine Sands. He was Chief Engineer at Leyland Motors and raced the Leyland Eight at Brooklands Racing circuit. He worked on the car, improved the streamlining and the engine, and started winning races. By 1923 he had left his job to concentrate on racing. He made further modifications to his car, which became the Leyland-Thomas, and on 26 June 1924 broke the world land speed record at Brooklands at 129.73mph. By September, it had been broken again by Malcolm Campbell on Pendine Sands. Thomas wanted the record back and purchased a 1923 Higham Special that had belonged to the racing driver Count Louis Zborowski, who had died in a crash at Monza during the Italian Grand Prix of 1924. He re-built and modified it, keeping its original aero engine, and named it 'Babs'. He shattered the record on Pendine Sands on 29 April 1926 when he reached 171.02mph. But Campbell was back at Pendine in February 1927 with his latest 'Bluebird' and re-took the record with 174.883mph.

On 3 March 1927, Thomas died on the sands when 'Babs' crashed. His attempt on the record was going well, the car was performing as it should have, but just near the completion of the mile it skidded, rolled, then righted itself. But Thomas had died the instant it rolled. He was 42.

This was the last time a land speed record was ever attempted on these sands.

The car was dragged away into the dunes and buried until in 1969, a North Wales Engineering lecturer called Owen Wyn Owyn got permission to recover it. It was in surprisingly good condition but all of the aluminium parts had rotted. Owyn spent a considerable amount of time restoring 'Babs'. It is now part of a permanent exhibition in the Museum of Speed at Pendine.

THE BASICS

Distance: 2 miles/3.2km
Gradient: Flat
Severity: Easy
Time: 1 hr
Stiles: None
Map: OS Explorer 177 (Carmarthen and Kidwelly)
Path description: Mostly sandy beach. Some pavement.
Start point: Beach Car Park at Pendine (GR SN 235080)
Parking: Beach Car Park at Pendine (charges apply) (SA33 4NY)
Landscape: Coast and sand dunes
Dog friendly: From May to September the beach is a dog-free zone
Toilets: Near the car park in the village
Nearest food: Barnacle Café just off the car park

PENDINE WALK

1. Exit the car park in the direction of the beach. Go up some steps then bear left to visit the Museum of Speed (free admission). Leave the Museum, still heading towards the beach, turn right then left down the slipway beside Barnacles Café. Keep walking across the sand and if the tide is out go down to where the sand is smooth and solid.

2. Turn left and walk along this flat, sandy beach. Continue for about a mile and look how much time it takes you. Then imagine the speed of those massive racing cars that used to power along here. At 160mph they would cover the same distance in less than 30 seconds.

3. When you see a line of telegraph poles on the dunes to your left start heading towards them. Then make for a lane that heads up onto the dunes at an angle. When you reach here you will see MOD signs warning you to keep out: sound advice because all of the area along the dunes here is an MOD firing range.

4. Turn left and walk along the beach above the high water mark. Now is the time for a spot of beachcombing. Kids just love this and will enjoy collecting shells, interestingly shaped pieces of driftwood, strands of rope and coloured stones. It's amazing the wonderful art they can produce from what they collect, like this amazing mermaid.

5. When you have walked back to the point where you entered the beach turn up past the Barnacle Café again then left beyond it and head along the promenade into the village. Turn right at the end and right again when you reach the road. You will pass several eating places and then arrive back at the entrance to the car park.

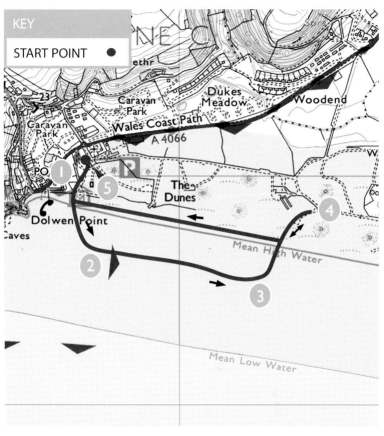

LLANSTEFFAN

A PLEASANT VILLAGE ASSOCIATED WITH THE POET DYLAN THOMAS, A LONG, SANDY BEACH, WOODLANDS, LOTS OF HISTORY AND SPLENDID VIEWS ARE THE ATTRACTIONS ON THIS WALK.

The remains of the 12th-century Norman Castle dominate the skyline from the top of Castle Hill but the Normans were relative latecomers to this corner of Wales. The ramparts of an Iron Age hill fort are still visible, indicating the strategic importance of this site about two-and-a-half millennia ago, guarding the Tywi estuary. Llansteffan grew around these fortifications and by the medieval period it was on a well-trodden pilgrimage route and was developing as a trading and fishing port. Cockle picking, fishing from coracles and seine net fishing were all practised here and many of these ancient crafts survived until quite recently.

By Victorian times it was a favourite holiday resort for the miners from the South Wales valleys, during the annual 'Miners' Fortnight'. The town was alive for two weeks with concerts and merriment, and locals capitalised by taking in holiday boarders. The holidaymakers came in paddle steamers or by rail. You can see the line of the Great Western Railway, designed by Isambard Kingdom Brunel, across the estuary. From there visitors took the ferry across the river.

Dylan Thomas knew that ferry well as he travelled back and forth. In his childhood and teens, Dylan Thomas spent a lot of his time in this area living with his Aunt Ann and her husband Jim Williams on their farm at Fern Hill, which is a few miles north of the village. One of his most famous poems is 'Fern Hill'. When his aunt died in February 1933 he wrote a poem called 'After the Funeral (In Memory of Ann Jones)'. She is buried near the chapel in the next village north, Llanybri. Buried close to her is the poet, Lynette Roberts, who was married to Thomas's friend Keidrych Rhys, editor of the magazine Wales. It was through Thomas that they came to live near the church at Llanybri, where they married in 1939 with Dylan as best man.

Another friend of Dylan Thomas, the novelist Glyn Jones, who had been born and brought up in Llansteffan, returned often after he had departed to Cardiff for a career as a teacher. The pair would meet other friends and repair to The Sticks for drinks. When Jones died he was buried in Llansteffan churchyard.

THE BASICS

Distance: 2 miles / 3.72km
Gradient: A couple of slight gradients. Mainly flat
Severity: Easy
Time: 1½ hrs
Stiles: Two
Map: OS Explorer 177 (Carmarthen and Kidwelly)
Path description: Beach, footpaths, lane and roads
Start point: Beach car park at Llansteffan (GR SN 353105)
Parking: Beach car park at Llansteffan (SA33 5LW)
Landscape: Coast, hills, village, woodland and fields
Dog friendly: No. Dogs are prohibited on the first part of the walk between May and September. Then there are stiles
Toilets: At the second car park along from the Beach Shop and Tea Room
Nearest food: Beach Shop and Tea Room and the Post Office and Tea Room

1. Leave the car park and walk towards the beach. Cross a tarmac footpath and continue onto the beach. Turn right and walk along it in the direction of the castle.

2. Towards the end of this bay turn right to go up some steps towards the last of a row of houses. Cross the path again then head across the car park towards the Beach Shop and Tea Room, then bear left to go onto a narrow footpath that heads uphill signposted for the castle.

3. When you reach the top of this go left onto a lane and follow it until it reaches a fork. Keep right then almost immediately bear left onto a footpath that goes through the woods. This has waymarkers for the Wales Coast Path. When it reaches a junction keep right passing a very musical bench. Keep following the coastal path, passing an area with a picnic table, bench and interpretation board.

4. Shortly after this the path forks. Take the right-hand path which is much narrower and heads uphill into the woods. Continue along this to reach a T-junction with a broader path and turn right onto it. Go through a gate, continue uphill and go through another gate by a cottage.

5. Turn right here although you may wish to stop and look at the stall with a range of homemade jams and preserves, which you can purchase and leave the money in an honesty box. Then continue on the road until it approaches a right-hand bend.

6. Bear left here to cross a stile then follow the wall on your left-hand side and after that the fence along woodland. When the fence turns sharply left keep ahead to reach a track and turn left along it. Then cross a stile and turn right onto a lane.

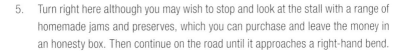

KEY

START POINT ●

Llansteffan

Follow this to reach the road into the village and turn left, then head downhill. Pass the church where the novelist and friend of Dylan Thomas Gwyn Jones is buried. Then pass the Sticks Hotel where the two of them would meet for drinks. Pass the Post Office and Café then look out for a footpath sign on the opposite side of the road by a green kissing gate.

7. Turn right onto the path. When it ends turn left then immediately right onto the road which will lead in a short distance to the entrance to the car park.

CARREG CENNEN

THIS WALK TAKES YOU BY A MAGNIFICENT HILLTOP CASTLE, THROUGH A SWEEPING VALLEY, WOODLANDS AND MEADOWS AND ENDS IN AN 11TH-CENTURY LONGHOUSE.

Carreg Cennen Castle, standing on its high hilltop, is one of the most impressive castle remains in Wales. Unsurprisingly, given its commanding position, fortifications here go back to the Iron Age, two-and-a-half thousand years ago; it was used by the Romans; and this building dates to the late 13th century when Edward I directed the building of castles all over Wales. It changed hands many times as it was besieged and fought over, until finally it was effectively demolished in 1462 at the end of the Wars of the Roses; the incumbents chose the Lancastrian side and the Yorkists won; they decided that it was too dangerous a stronghold to leave intact and had it demolished.

However, the remains still reveal a great deal about the shape of the buildings and life within its walls. If you make the climb to the castle you will realise just how difficult entry would have been to an invader. If you do not suffer from claustrophobia, investigate the steep steps down to the cave beneath the rock. Somewhere in a cavern down there, according to legend, lies Owain Lawgoch, the last true Prince of Wales, with his warriors, awaiting the call from the Welsh to liberate Wales from the Saxon invader.

Most of the buildings around were built using recycled stone from the castle. The exception is the 11th-century longhouse at the farm, which obviously pre-dates the demolition. Whatever you do, do not miss this building, with its ramshackle but fascinating display of farm implements and information about their uses. Originally thatched and now slated, it is divided within into three sections, the store for machinery and implements, the cattle stalls and the living quarters. This is a design which would have been found all over medieval Europe, although many of the buildings would have been wattle and daub rather than stone. The implements on display, of course, are not 11th century.

They are from a more recent bygone age of rakes and butter churns and mangles, but no less interesting for that. If you visit in summer you will find it full of swallows' nests, and in late summer the young birds swoop and dive around you as you explore.

THE BASICS

Distance: 2 miles / 3.2km

Gradient: Fairly steep

Severity: Moderate

Time: 1½ hrs

Stiles: Four with dog gates

Map: OS Explorer 186 (Llandeilo and Brechfa Forest)

Path description: Grassy or stony paths and road

Start point: Car park at Carreg Cenen Catle (GR SN 666193)

Parking: Carreg Cennen Castle Car Park, just east of Trapp (SA19 6UA)

Landscape: Hills and valleys

Dog friendly: Yes, but on leads near livestock

Toilets: At the car park

Nearest food: Tearoom next to the car park

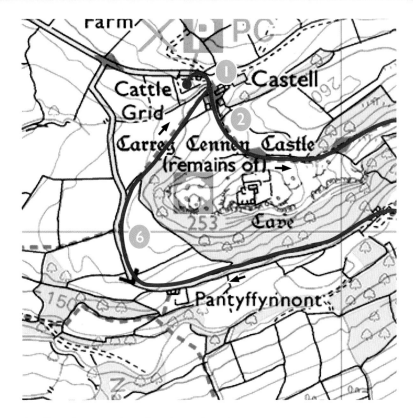

1. From the car park go through a gate and along the path to the tearoom, visitor centre and longhouse. Pass through the buildings straight ahead towards the castle. Wind uphill to the entrance to the castle at a gate and a wooden booth. Turn left to go through a gate then follow the waymarkers for the red and yellow castle walks.

2. Follow a grassy path downhill with a sweeping valley to your right and hills in the distance ahead. At the bottom of the hill you will come to a dog-leg turn to the right and a bridge over the river, signposted for the red castle walk.

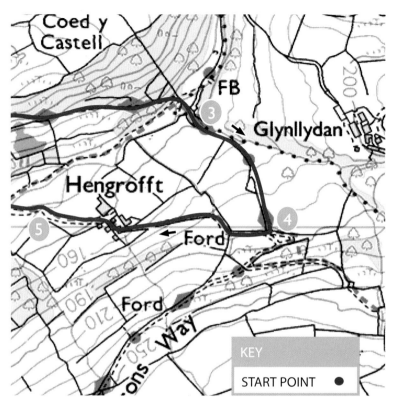

Coed y
Castell

FB

Glynllydan

Hengrofft

200

Ford

160

190

210

Ford

Way

250

ons

KEY

START POINT ●

3. Cross the bridge and follow the path bearing left away from the river. The path continues between high hedges of hawthorn, hazel and oak, crossing several stiles and eventually reaching a stile to a farm road. The red castle walk signpost points ahead but you are turning right here onto the farm road.

4. Wind down the road, through a farm steading with the castle now ahead of you. Continue on this farm track until you reach a country lane. Turn left onto the lane.

5. You are now re-joining the yellow castle walk. Continue on this for some time until

you reach a footpath on the right. Go through a gate then head uphill through a meadow to return to the start.

6. When you reach the visitor centre, make sure that you look at the longhouse, then make your way back to the car park.

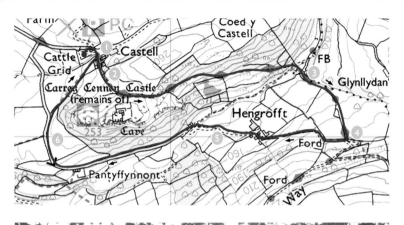

LLANDEILO

MEANDER ROUND THIS PRETTY LITTLE TOWN LOOKING AT HISTORICAL BUILDINGS RANGING FROM THE MEDIEVAL TO THE GEORGIAN. THEN ENJOY A NATURE STROLL THROUGH THE PLANNED LANDSCAPE OF A RICH MAN'S PARK AND VISIT AN ABANDONED CHURCHYARD THAT WOULD NOT BE OUT OF PLACE IN A HORROR FILM.

Llandeilo owes its name to St Teilo, a 6th-century saint and contemporary of St David, the patron Saint of Wales. It started as a small religious community but by the 9th century was the seat of the Bishop of St Teilo, had two stone crosses and was the home of the St Teilo Gospels. Much earlier than this Llandeilo was probably a blip on the road that linked the forts at Loughor with the one in Dinefwr Park and there would have been a crossing point, of sorts, on the River Towy near here. In medieval times a bridge spanned the river downstream of the current one. It was of stone construction with seven pointed arches and the remains can still be viewed. Its central section was badly damaged in a flood in 1795 but it continued in use, shored up with wooden supports. The great landscape painter, Turner, depicted this on one of his canvases. Work on the current bridge was put out to tender in 1843 and the work awarded to the lowest bidder. The bid was unrealistic and during construction the County Bridge Supervisor died and the budget was spent with only a third of the work done. The contractor was sacked and a new one appointed with the ultimate price on completion soaring to over three times the original estimate. When it was finally opened in 1848 locals named it 'The Bridge of Sighs' but it was a masterpiece. With a span of 145 feet (44m) it was the third largest in Britain at the time and considered one of the Wonders of Wales.

Penlan Park, designed by the local architect and surveyor W.D. Jenkins, is on land gifted to the townspeople by Lord Dynevor in 1908. Sitting high above the Towy valley it has magnificent views across the surrounding countryside.

The land here was originally part of the Dinfwr Park, a designed landscape that you briefly enter as part of this walk. Should you want to explore it further you will find two Roman forts, a medieval castle, the remains of two medieval townships and much else of interest.

THE BASICS

Distance: 2¼miles / 3.6km
Gradient: A couple of very short climbs. Otherwise flat
Severity: Easy
Time: 1½ to 2hrs
Stiles: None
Map: OS Explorer 186 (Llandeilo and Brecha Forest)
Path description: Pavements, well-surfaced tracks and footpaths and rough footpath through woodland
Start point: Municipal car park in Llandeilo (GR SN 630224)
Parking: Municipal car park in Llandeilo town centre (charges apply) (SA19 6HJ)
Landscape: Town, woodland, valley park and river
Dog friendly: Yes, but keep on lead when advised
Toilets: At car park
Nearest food: Café Braz in King Street

LLANDEILO WALK

1. Exit the car park towards Crescent Road. At the junction is the Civic Hall, built in 1887 to commemorate Queen Victoria's Golden Jubilee. Turn right into the Crescent. Next to the Civic Hall is Capel Newydd, dating from the opening years of the 20th century. Further along the street is the Italian Romanesque architecture of the Ebenezer Baptist Chapel, which was built in 1877.

2. Turn right into Abbey Terrace and walk along to the junction and turn left into Bridge Street. The large building on the corner of George Street and Bridge Street was the King's Head, an 18th-century coaching inn. The mock timber framing is a 20th-century addition. Continue along down Bridge Street to the bridge then turn right onto a lane that leads to the river.

3. Walk along to a gate at the entrance to Castle Woods. Go through a kissing gate and walk along a well-surfaced footpath. Soon after passing a wooden ramp on your right you reach a junction. Bear left and follow the path to visit the abandoned church of Llandyfeisant.

4. Leave the churchyard and return to the ramp and head up it. Climb for a short section then a path heads round the contours of the hill passing through woods. There's a steep drop on the left-hand side. Soon the path climbs again to some steps towards the end. Go through a metal kissing gate then keep left, uphill on steps to reach a tarmac path. Turn right onto this and follow it through the rest of the park.

5. Exit the park onto Carmarthen Street. On the right, next to the park entrance is the former National School, now a nursery. Next door is what was the headmaster's house, built in the 1850s. Across the street is the derelict-looking Provisions Market which was built in 1838. Proceed down the street then turn right into George Street. As George Street runs into King Street, head right into Bank Terrace and have a look at the old bank. This started in 1842 as the Bank of the Black Ox, for the cattle drovers who regularly passed through the town.

6. Return to King Street and at the bottom turn right into a landscaped area, then through a gap in the hedge to enter the churchyard. During the 17th century this was a marketplace with the tombstones used as stalls. Underneath two copper

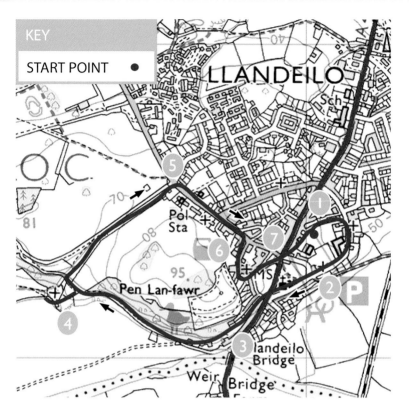

KEY

START POINT ●

LLANDEILO

beech trees near the back you will find the memorial stone to the 'Leonardo of Llandeilo', Thomas Jenkins, whose diaries provide a fascinating insight into town life between 1826 and 1871.

7. Leave the churchyard, cross the street and enter the grounds of St Teilo's Church. All that remains of the medieval church is the tower. The rest is 19th century. Inside are copies of the St Teilo Gospel. The original is in Lichfield Cathedral. Exit the churchyard via a gate on the opposite side and turn right down Church Street, passing the well set into the wall. Then keep going to the junction and turn right to head uphill. Passing into Rhosmaen Street you can see on the left the Cawdor Arms, an early 18th-century building, previously the Bear Inn. Through an archway just beyond the hotel is the Horeb Wesleyan Chapel built behind the inn in 1810. Across the road from this in Rhosmaen Alley is a Calvinist Methodist Chapel, built in 1788. Continue along the street from here, then shortly turn into an entrance that takes you past public toilets into the rear of the car park.

GORSLAS

Llyn Llech Owain Country Park is a great day out for all the family. Wonderful scenery, lots of wildlife and a legend thrown in for good measure.

Legend has it that this is called Owain's Lake after one of King Arthur's knights, who was responsible for its creation. The story goes that there was a mountain, Mynydd Mawr, above what is the present town of Gorslas. Local shepherds toiled here to make a living because of the rough grazing and absence of water. Then one day one of them came across a strange stone, carved with mysterious symbols. Soon he and his companions had dislodged the stone from the ground and were amazed when water started gushing out. This startled them and made them drop the stone. As soon as they did the flow of water stopped. They figured magic was afoot but used it to their advantage by occasionally raising the stone to let out enough water for their stock and to irrigate the land. Soon it became fertile and the shepherds prospered.

Meanwhile King Arthur was sending his knights off to find the Holy Grail. One of the knights, Sir Owain, came to this area, where he found his way barred by a knight on horseback and with crossed hands on his shield. He demanded money to let Sir Owain pass and a fight ensued. Sir Owain slew his adversary but was seriously wounded himself. He hauled himself onto his horse and uttered one word: 'water'. He lost consciousness and when he awoke, he was on top of the hill next to the shepherd's stone, bearing the words 'The Magic Well of Gorslas'.

He used his remaining strength to move it, drank his fill and then lost consciousness again to dream of rising waters and lakes. When he awoke again he was on an island. So he swam for the shore, where he encountered the irate shepherds. Owain confessed that he had left the well unstopped but pointed out that they now had a lake and in time would be able to get fish from it. This pleased the shepherds and they were even more delighted to learn that Owain had slain the knight, who had terrorised them for years. And that is why to this day this is called Owain's Lake.

THE BASICS

Distance: 2½ miles / 4km

Gradient: Flat

Severity: Easy

Time: 1½ to 2 hrs

Stiles: None

Map: OS Explorer 178 (Llanelli and Ammanford)

Path description: Well-surfaced footpaths

Start point: Llyn Llech Owain Country Park (GR SN 565148)

Parking: At the Country Park, just north of Gorslas between the A48 and A476 (charges apply) (SA14 7NG)

Landscape: Lake, peat bog, heathland and forest

Dog friendly: Yes

Toilets: At café beside car park and in visitor centre

Nearest food: Café beside car park

GORSLAS WALK

1. From the car park head towards the café
    and then pass to the right of it, heading
    along a footpath that runs to the left of a
    children's adventure play area. At the first
    two junctions bear left. The lake will now
    come into view on your right. Keep on the
    footpath as the ground can be rather boggy
    round this part. Eventually you will see
    ahead of you a building that resembles a
    giant dovecote. This is the visitor centre.
    Cross an area of duckboarding then climb
    some stairs to reach the entrance. Head
    inside and enjoy the panoramic views of
    the lake from the viewing galleries on both
    floors. Scientists have discovered that there
    are some 25 feet of peat and lake muds that
    have built up here since the last Ice Age, and
    through analysis they were able to form the
    conclusion that the lake was first formed
    around 15,000 to 19,000 years ago. During
    World War II the German Luftwaffe used this lake as a direction finder during their
    bombing runs to hit Liverpool and the English Midlands. The moon reflecting on the
    water surface gave them the navigational fix they needed to continue to their targets.

2. Head past the centre, going through a kissing gate to the side of a large wooden
    one. Keep ahead along a well-surfaced footpath, turning briefly to the right to go
    out onto a bridge to a pumping tower for more views along the lake. Then return to
    the footpath. Keep on this path, following the waymarkers for the red route, passing
    a wooden hide on the left, going though a crossroads then turning right at the next
    junction where a dirt footpath continues straight ahead into the woods. Look out for
    the red kite, one of the rarest birds of prey in the UK.

3. Keep on the red route as the path turns right again to pass a field that usually has
    lots of Exmoor ponies in it on the left. These are used as 'conservation grazers'
    to help manage the habitat. By eating the purple moorgrass and scrub they allow
    more heather to grow. Over to your right you will see the lake and in the distance
    the distinctive visitor centre. When you reach a gate, go through it, then turn left.
    Continue to another crossroads and turn left here onto a footpath with a blue
    waymarker that initially goes through some woodland.

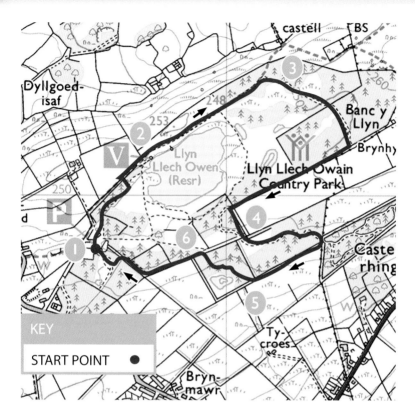

4. When you reach a junction, turn right as indicated by another blue waymarker. This narrower path will continue along open ground before entering further woodland. When you reach a junction turn left back onto a footpath and keep following the blue route. When you reach a junction ignore the right turn for the car park and take the left fork.

5. Then turn left onto a path with a green waymarker and a bird symbol. Follow this path through the woods, keeping left at a junction to arrive at a bird hide with grand views over a secluded little lake. Then retrace your steps to the main path and turn left.

6. Keep on this as it twists and turns, following signs for the car park. Eventually arrive at the rear of the park to the left of the children's play park.

CILYCWM

THIS WALK STARTS FROM A PICTURESQUE VILLAGE WITH A MEDIEVAL CHURCH, PASSES BY A GRADE II LISTED METHODIST CHAPEL AND MEANDERS BACK BY LOVELY WOODLAND WITH VIEWS OVER PASTORAL HILLS AND VALLEY.

The famous 18th-century writer of hymns, William Williams Pantycelyn, was a member of Soar Chapel, also known as Tynewydd Chapel, which you pass on the walk. He wrote mainly in his native Welsh and his most famous hymn was 'Arglwydd awain trwy'r anialwych', which translates as 'Guide Me O Thou Great Redeemer'; still sung fervently in Wales to the tune of 'Cwm Rhondda'. The first chapel built on this site in 1740 was one of the first Methodist chapels in Wales. The building still standing was built in 1786.

© Stuart Wilding

William Williams had intended to become a doctor but after hearing an evangelical preacher in 1737, he determined to devote his life to religion and travelled for miles around the country preaching. He would have attended both of the chapels here as a member and as an itinerant preacher. He was born near Beulah in 1716 and for much of his life he lived at Llanfair-ar-bryn, near Llandovery. He is buried in the churchyard at Llandovery. He gained the nickname or bardic name Pantycelyn from the name of his father's farm. It was a common practice in Wales, where surnames are often patronymic, and so are shared by many people, to add another distinguishing name. Williams was also known as Y per ganiedydd or the Sweet Songster on account of his beautiful hymns.

The other church in Cilycwm is the early 14th-century St Michael's in the centre of the village. As you look through the lychgate you see a particularly well-proportioned tower, which was added to the original church, probably late in the 14th century. Go inside to see the beautiful barrel-vaulted roof and the original massive stone arcades. Look at the pillar to the right of the door, which is undercut to make space for a stone font. No one knows whether this was an original feature but it certainly appears to be. Make sure you have a look at the 18th-century wall paintings, once painted over in the 1980s. Before you leave have a look around the churchyard at the old yew trees, one of which is purported to be 1,500 years old.

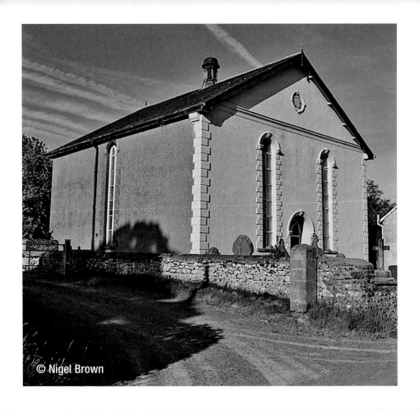

© Nigel Brown

THE BASICS

Distance: 2¼ miles / 4km

Gradient: A few moderate slopes

Severity: Moderate

Time: 2 hrs

Stiles: One

Map: OS Explorer 187 (Llandovery)

Path description: Road, woodland and grassy paths but likely to be muddy at all times. Don't attempt this walk without stout waterproof boots

Start point: The church at Cilycwm (GR SN 753400)

Parking: On the street in Cilycwm, to the north of Llandovery (SA20 0ST)

Landscape: Woodland and fields

Dog friendly: Yes but must be on lead near livestock

Toilets: None

Nearest food: Neuadd Fawr Arms in the village

CILYCWM WALK

1. From the church, walk along the main street to the turning signposted for Cynghordy and turn into that road. Continue on this country lane between hedges. As it winds uphill the view of the surrounding hills opens up before you. You will pass Pen y Fedw Farm on your left and then reach Soar Chapel.

© Trevor Rickard

2. Have a look at the chapel and the graveyard and the school building behind it and then continue on the road as it winds downhill to a bridge over the river. Do not cross the bridge but look for two gates to your right. Go through the right-hand gate, marked with a footpath sign. The path is grassy but uneven.

3. Almost immediately you reach a fork. Take the level path to the left to a gate. Go through the gate and follow a grassy path bearing right uphill to a wood. At the top go through a gate onto a level but uneven grassy path through woods alongside open fields. You will reach a gate onto a farm track. Go through the gate, cross the farm track and go through the gate opposite to continue ahead.

4. This path through woods is alternately grassy and muddy and you will go through several gates until you come to a crossroads at a farm. The very short part from the last gate to the farm can be quite overgrown.

5. After the farm continue ahead along the farm road then just before it bends to cross the river turn right through a gate with a yellow waymarker on the post and walk round the left-hand side of the field until you reach a metal gate. Go through it and bear left to go through another a few feet away. Turn left and cross a track to go through a third gate.

6. Now walk across a field with the river on your left, go through a gate at the end of this field and keep straight ahead. There is little sign of a footpath here but a right of way does exist. Follow the yellow waymark arrows where you can, although many are broken or missing. Go through the next gate and keep ahead, making towards a house on the horizon.

7. Then go through one final gate. Follow a footpath round to the right, then left into a field, still by the river. Veer slightly to the right across this field and cross over a stile on the wall to reach the lane you went along on the outward part of the walk.

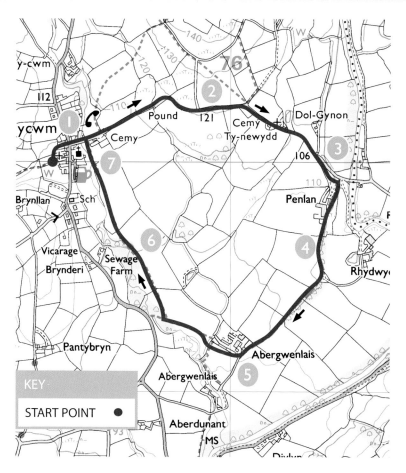

Turn left and retrace your steps to the start.

© Nigel Brown

LLANDOVERY

UNEARTH THE STORY OF A LEGENDARY WELSH HERO, THEN FOLLOW THE TRAIL OF THE OLD CATTLE DROVERS TO DISCOVER THE ORIGINS OF WELSH BANKING.

Llywelyn Ap Gruffydd Fuchan

When the Welsh rose against the English, under Owen Glyndŵr in the War of Liberation in the early 15th century, Glyndŵr and his men sacked and burned the English colonial towns and castles and created a Welsh Parliament. But Henry IV of England invaded Wales with a huge army containing the most battle-hardened troops in Europe. Glyndŵr was declared an outlaw and fled into hiding. He was never betrayed by his people. The English seized local landowner Llywelyn ap Gruffydd Fychan and demanded that he lead them to Glyndŵr. Llywelyn had two sons fighting with Glyndŵr and so led the English on a futile hunt for several weeks. Henry smelt a rat and had him tortured. When he still refused to betray Glyndŵr, Henry had him publicly hanged, drawn and quartered in the centre of Llandovery. In the dying years of the 20th century a local campaign was started to erect a monument to his memory. It was unveiled in 2001 and dominates the car park at the start of the walk. The 16-foot (5m) tall stainless steel statue, standing on a rock just under the castle, depicts the empty helmet and cloak of a knight with lance and shield.

Llandovery was an important staging point on many of the old droving routes and at its peak would see 30,000 cattle pass through en route to London each year. One of the drovers, David Jones, founded his own bank in Llandovery, in 1799, using the profits from his business and his wife's dowry. He called his new establishment David Jones and Co, but as he adopted the image of a Black Ox to print on his bank notes, the bank became known as The Black Ox. This bank started life in the building now occupied by The Kings Head in Market Square. Jones was successful in his venture and soon opened branches in other Welsh towns. The bank continued as a family business after his death and was ultimately run by his grandson before becoming part of Lloyds Bank in 1909. Even then the trusted Black Ox symbol survived on local chequebooks until 1929. If you go to Lloyds Bank in Llandovery you will still see David Jones's initials over the door.

THE BASICS

Distance: 2¾ miles / 4.4km

Gradient: A couple of slight gentle gradients

Severity: Easy

Time: 2 hrs

Stiles: Eight

Map: OS Explorer 187 (Llandovery)

Path description: Good surfaced footpaths, rougher footpaths, fields, lanes and pavements

Start point: Car park in Llandovery town centre (GR SN 767342)

Parking: In Llandovery town centre near the Tourist Information Centre (SA20 0AW)

Landscape: Riverside, hills, fields and town

Dog friendly: No

Toilets: At car park

Nearest food: Cafe West End or the Drovers Diner on the High Street

1. Leave the car park and go onto the footpath that runs past the castle and the impressive statue of Llywelyn ap Gruffydd Fychan. When the path forks bear right uphill onto a narrower footpath, which continues to Waterloo Bridge. Then climb a set of steps to reach the road.

2. Turn left onto Waterloo Street and pass the red-brick barn that was once the Jubilee Stores of T. Roberts, a merchant and ironmonger. At the junction turn right into High Street, then cross the road and continue to cross a junction with Gellideg and then the front of the Kings Arms.

3. As the pavement rises to cross a bridge, keep left in front of some houses, passing a set of steps on your right, to reach a footpath sign by the river. Turn left here and proceed along the riverside path although it will still be some time before you actually get a glimpse of the water. Go through a kissing gate and veer right to continue on the riverside path. Now you will see it over the wall. The path widens to a track and when it turns right and starts heading uphill to a gate, keep left to walk along a footpath that passes the end of some gardens.

4. When you come to a stile crossing to the right, ignore it, turn left, then right when you reach a street and follow it as it turns to the left. Keep to the right-hand side to reach a footpath sign just before a post box, then bear right onto a pavement in front of some houses, then enter a small park with a children's play area. Keep to the well-paved path to reach a gap where a gate used to be at a junction with the main road. Carefully cross this, bearing right to head uphill on a B road. As you near the top of the hill Llanfair Church comes into view on the right. On the road opposite it look out for a footpath fingerpost then turn left over a stile. Although this has a dog gate the next few don't.

5. Walk downhill on a faint grass footpath heading for the right-hand side of some trees. Then cross another stile, veer right to cross a third and head up a set of steps to reach the railway line. Take great care crossing here then go down more steps and over a fourth stile and veer left to a fifth stile in the corner of this field. Strangely this one also has a dog gate. Keep ahead following a more visible grass footpath to reach one more stile (no dog gate) and beyond it a broad track.

6. Turn left along the track, then immediately left again to walk to the right of some trees. This will bring you out just beyond a seriously tumbledown footbridge. Proceed from there to a gate where you cross a stile then turn right onto a lane. Proceed along this for a few hundred yards until it starts to bend right. Then cross the road and take a left turn down a narrower lane beside Brookdale.

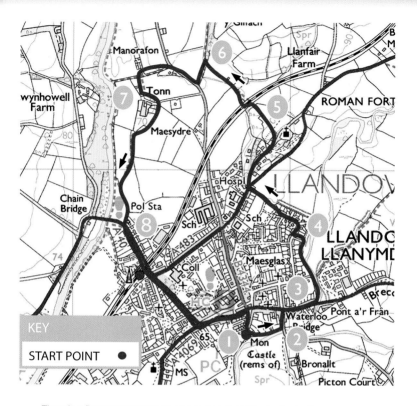

There is a fingerpost but it is broken and partly hidden by the hedge.

7. Before the lane turns left to go over a bridge, turn left to cross a footbridge. Then go through a kissing gate, follow the hedge on your right to go through another kissing gate, cross a lane and through a third then continue, still keeping to the tree line on your right. When you see a black barn head towards it then turn right in front of it to go through a kissing gate, turn left and continue along a visible grassy path. At the next gate cross a stile and veer right onto a more visible path that now runs to the right of a hedgerow. After the next kissing gate veer left and keep following the fence, then go through another kissing gate and along a short section of footpath to go through one final kissing gate onto the road.

8. Turn left and head back into town passing a police station on your left, re-crossing the railway, keeping left to go along Queensway past the college then turn left at a junction into Broad Street. Pass the Caffi West End and then the War Memorial. To the left is Market Square. Cross the road and walk along the side of the Castle Hotel then turn right to reach the statue of a drover. Pass the tourist office and re-enter the car park.

LLANELLI

IT IS HARD TO BELIEVE AS YOU WALK ALONG THE SHORE
AND AROUND THIS PEACEFUL LAKE THAT THIS WAS A HUGE
INDUSTRIAL SITE. THE LAKE WAS A COOLING LAKE FOR THE
STEELWORKS THAT STOOD NEARBY, BUT NOWADAYS YOU
SHOULD REMEMBER TO TAKE SOMETHING TO FEED THE
DUCKS AND SWANS.

The Llanelli Steel Works, later the Duport Steel Works, was one of the largest and most modern in the world by the time it closed. It opened in 1897 and was known locally as the 'Klondike' because, as the workers were so much better paid than anywhere else, there was a 'gold rush' to work there. Unfortunately, like so much of the industrial base of the country, it closed down in the 1980s and Llanelli was left with unemployment and an industrial wasteland, where there had been prosperity. There are few reminders of the past but as you walk around the lake look for the black stones, once molten and seething with bubbles. These are waste from the furnaces, which once boiled them and spat them out.

The local council acquired the site and with help of the Welsh Development Agency they have transformed it into this pleasant park, so that now the town looks straight out to sea with a view unimpeded by factories. Tourism has replaced the industry of the past and there is much to see. The bay here is home to many seabirds including overwintering common Scoters, while the saltmarshes and mud flats are a rich habitat for oystercatchers, wigeon, knot and pintail among a whole range of waders and wildfowl. The clean waters of the bay also attract fish such as salmon and sea trout.

THE BASICS

Distance: 2½ miles / 4km

Gradient: Negligible

Severity: Easy

Time: 1¼ hrs

Stiles: None

Map: OS Explorer 178 (Llanelli & Ammanford)

Path description: Tarmac path

Start point: Discovery Centre car park (GR SS 497993)

Parking: Discovery Centre, North Dock, Llanelli (SA15 2LF)

Landscape: Coast and lakeside

Dog friendly: Yes

Toilets: At Discovery Centre

Nearest food: Restaurant at Discovery Centre

LLANELLI WALK

1. From the car park walk past the Discovery Centre towards the shore and take the coastal path. Follow the fingerpost to Sandy Water Park along the shore. Shortly after an open area with benches and a sculpture of a cormorant, take a fork to the left, leading up to a tall steel monument.

2. This is the Millennium Monument. From here bear right towards a block monument on a slight rise ahead. This memorial has information about the steelworks and the regeneration of the area as a park. Go left from here on a path downhill to reach the lake. Turn right and walk along the lakeside. At the first turn there is a feeding point for ducks and swans and they mass here in expectation in the water and on the path. As you go on round the next turn, you will find a feeding station for you – a pub – on the right.

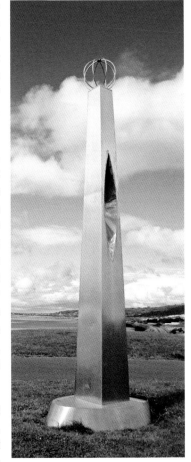

3. Continue keeping the lake on your left until you reach a narrow wooden bridge. Turn left over the bridge and go left at the path crossroads and head back along the lake until you see some standing stones on your right.

4. Cut across the grass to have a look at the standing stones. Children will enjoy climbing on them. From here go on up the hill to reach the block on the hill again. Go back downhill. If you have time you can divert to the woods to the left and have a look round the Mabinogion sculpture trail within.

5. Either way retrace your steps along the paths back to the car park.

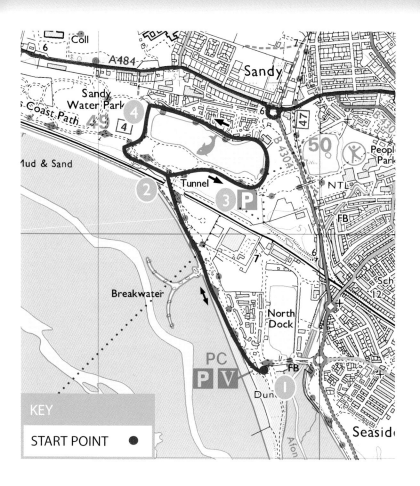

KEY

START POINT •

PEMBREY

Another wonderful walk through land reclaimed from Carmarthenshire's Industrial past. It is difficult to imagine that this tranquil park was once one of the most dangerous areas in all of Wales for it was here that gunpowder was manufactured from the late 19th century.

By the Second World War, Pembrey was the country's largest producer of the explosive compound trinitrotoluene (TNT), turning out 700 tons of the stuff every single week. After the war, production continued on a small scale but the factory was more involved in removing TNT from obsolete bombs and surplus ammunition. It also manufactured ammonium nitrate for use as a fertiliser. Although it had been winding down for a long time it was not finally closed until 1962.

The sand dunes of Pembrey Burrow were the ideal site for explosives manufacture. It was remote, the dunes provided a natural barrier should any explosions occur and it was relatively easy to create subterranean bunkers.

While gunpowder had been made here for some time it was not until the First World War that the facility took off. The government had the Glasgow-based Nobel Explosive Company build and run a factory for the production of TNT. The government put up the money for the construction and retained ownership while Nobel operated it. Like many similar munitions works it was run down and closed shortly after the war, but was re-opened during the run-up to the Second World War. Most of the facility was rebuilt and it was renamed the Royal Ordnance Factory. Magazines, acid plants and nitration areas were constructed at a safe distance from the workers' facilities, accommodation and administrative buildings. Huge mounds and underground bunkers provided camouflage as well as safety. Railway lines ran throughout the site providing transport of raw materials and the completed ordnance.

The site had its own electrical generation facility, steam generating plant and water supply brought from two small rivers a few miles distant, stored, treated, filtered and distributed where it was required. The facility was to a great extent self-sufficient.

Most of the factory is gone but you can still come across traces as you explore. There are bits of railway line in front of the Adventure Play Area and a few of the bunkers can still be traced. Otherwise it is as if it was never here.

© Colin Bews

THE BASICS

Distance: 4 miles/ 6.4km
Gradient: Flat apart from one very short path up through the dunes at point 3
Severity: Easy
Time: 2 hrs
Stiles: None
Map: OS Explorer 178 (Llanelli and Ammanford)
Path description: Hard surfaced lanes and footpaths, sandy beach
Start point: Visitor Centre, Pembrey Country Park (GR SN 406005)
Parking: Pembrey Country Park (SA16 0EJ)
Landscape: Parkland, woodland and coast
Dog friendly: Very
Toilets: Near the beach at point 2
Nearest food: At the caravan area just beyond the Visitor Centre and as you reach the beach

1. Start from the Visitor Centre and head along the lane in the same direction as you entered the park. Ignoring junctions with other lanes continue by turning left, to pass a golfing area, then right to pass the hut where you can hire a Segway. The next junction to the right is for the miniature railway, but go left here instead, then right when you reach a T-junction. Take the first left to enter and cross another parking area (there's a telephone kiosk on your right here). Then cross to a path that passes to the right of two massive anchors that were found on Cefn Sidan beach. They are old Admiralty long-shank anchors and the fact they were found within 200 metres of each other with chains running at 45 degrees to the shore would indicate that they were bower anchors, put out by a ship of at least 1,000 tons that would have been in extreme difficulties at the time. Now keep ahead, passing the beach shop, café and toilets then onto the beach itself past the RNLI station.

2. Head down towards the water until you reach hard sand (at high tides you won't have this option) then turn right and walk along this long sandy beach. After about half a mile (1km) turn up towards the dunes making towards one of the red signs. The one you are looking for is numbered CE  58. Do not attempt to cross the dunes at any other point, as the going is very rough and hazardous.

3. Pass the sign onto a footpath that leads through the dunes then up some steps. At a junction keep right to reach the cycle path. Turn left onto this and head along it.

4. When you reach a junction beside a wooden bird hide turn left. Take some time to explore the hide, which has a superb view over a small pond teeming with wildlife. Then continue along the cycle track. There are small posters warning you to be aware of the Wild Parsnip, a common plant, which can cause a rash if touched. Children are particularly susceptible to this so keep them away from it. Shortly you will pass a junction on the right, which lets you have another view of the little lake. Then keep ahead on the cycle path.

5. When the path curves right and another path heads off into the woods keep right on the cycle path. There are various footpaths leading from this route and if you pick up a park map when you enter then you can explore them. Otherwise stick to

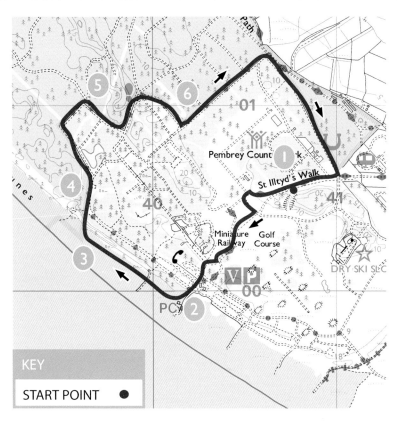

KEY

START POINT ●

this route. Pass marker posts with green and purple tops. First is the number 5 in purple. Then turn left at a T-junction and immediately pass another marker, then a short post with the number 6 in both green and purple. At the next junction when a faint footpath heads off to the left keep right as the main path curves round. Bear left at the next junction marked with a purple 7 and a post, then turn left at a T-junction.

6. Walk along a long straight section with the occasional orange-topped post. At the next T-junction go right. Then pass by a green metal gate and Pembrey Park Riding Centre. At the end of this road turn right at a T-junction to rejoin the main lane through the park and follow it back to the start.

© Humphrey Bolton

KIDWELLY

A FAIRLY STRENUOUS WALK EXPLORING THE COUNTRYSIDE ROUND KIDWELLY, AND THE STORY OF PRINCESS GWENLLIAN, THE WELSH BOADICEA. NOT FAR INTO THIS WALK YOU WILL VISIT KIDWELLY CASTLE, WHICH STARTED LIFE AS A 12TH-CENTURY FORTRESS CREATED AS PART OF THE NORMAN ATTEMPTS TO SUBDUE AND CONTROL THE WELSH.

There's a memorial stone just in front of the main entrance to the castle. This is dedicated to the memory of Princess Gwenllian. She was the wife of Gruffydd ap Rhys, Prince of Deheubarth in South Wales. In December 1135 Henry I died. The dispute over his succession led to a civil war that raged through England and Normandy from 1135 to 1154.

The Welsh took advantage of this to rise against the Normans and on New Year's Day 1136 defeated an Anglo-Norman army in battle near Swansea. Gruffydd ap Rhys then headed north to increase the size of his army. However, in his absence the Norman Lord of Kidwelli, Maurice de Londres, counter-attacked with a view to crushing the rebellion before it grew.

Princess Gwenllian and her two sons, Morgan and Maelgwn, raised what fighting forces they could to hold the position until her husband returned with reinforcements. She stood against the Normans in a field a mile outside Kidwelly but her resistance stood no chance against the battle-hardened Norman forces and she was defeated. Legend has it that she personally fought like a demon but was killed on the battlefield along with her son Morgan, her other son being executed by beheading after the battle. Other stories tell of her being captured alive then beheaded as a warning to others. Whatever the truth of it, for centuries tales were told on dark winter nights of a headless body that could be seen wandering Maes Gwenllian (Gwenllian's Field) or round the castle walls.

Gwenllian's patriotic stand and subsequent brutal death sparked off what has become known as The Great Revolt, as others in South Wales, inspired by her patriotism, rose against the hated Normans. 'Revenge for Gwenllian' was a popular battle cry of Welsh troops for many centuries after her death.

© Robin Drayton

THE BASICS

Distance: 5 miles / 8km

Gradient: A couple of steep inclines on the outward section

Severity: Strenuous

Time: 2½ to 3 hrs

Stiles: Two (gate beside one)

Map: OS Explorer 178 (Llanelli and Ammanford)

Path description: Well-surfaced footpaths, rocky footpaths, grass fields, lanes, tracks and pavement

Start point: Car park in Station Road in the centre of Kidwelly (GR SN 406067)

Parking: Car park in centre of the village on Station Road (SA17 4UH)

Landscape: Hills, valley, tidal estuary, woodland, farmland and town

Dog friendly: Yes, apart from possibly one stile

Toilets: At junction of Station Road and Bridge Street beside the Farmers Arms

Nearest food: Several options on Bridge Street

KIDWELLY WALK

1. Exit the car park and turn right into Station Road. Then at the junction turn left into Bridge Street and cross the bridge. In bygone times you would have needed to pay a toll to do this.

2. Turn right onto the riverside footpath with a fingerpost pointing to the castle. Pass the former Castle Mill, now an antiques business, go through a kissing gate, go along the walkway, then cross a footbridge and turn left uphill to visit the castle. Just in front of it is a memorial to Princess Gwenllian. After your visit go back down to the footbridge and continue along the riverside path. This will head away from the river and uphill to go through a kissing gate beside a play park. Keep straight ahead here to reach a road junction then turn right. Cross the road and turn right then head uphill. Look out for a junction just after the road bends right. It looks like the drive into houses but a wooden fingerpost indicating that this is the Summer Way will ensure you are on the right track.

3. Turn left to pass the sign then, ignoring the gate in front of you, bear right to go through a narrow gap in the hedge then head uphill on a delightful footpath between two hedges. This is a very rocky path so proceed with caution. The going is slow here as the path climbs the hillside. Then it turns to the right at another Summer Way sign and levels off.

4. The next section has a better surface and is almost level. Keep on it, enjoying brief glimpses of the valley below through gaps in the trees and hedgerow. Then go through three gates.

5. After the last gate the path heads uphill again and through another three gates. After the third, keep ahead, over grass, towards some trees. There is a faint but visible path but a straight line will take you to the next section. After the trees make straight towards a gate in the fence. Go through it onto a permissive route, bear right then cross a stile (a gate beside this can be opened for dogs). Then keep ahead on a short track to reach a junction with a lane.

6. Turn left and follow this all the way to Penlan Farm. Turn left just in front of the brown farmhouse then in a very short distance turn right onto a track with a Permissive Route marker. Please observe the instructions on various signs and keep your dog on a lead. Follow this track, past an insect hotel the farmer has built.

7. When the track turns to the right keep ahead to go through a gate following yellow waymarkers. Walk along the edge of this field keeping close to the hedge. Then go across a stile in the corner of the field and walk across the next field towards farm buildings. Go through a gate and turn left onto a track that runs up through the

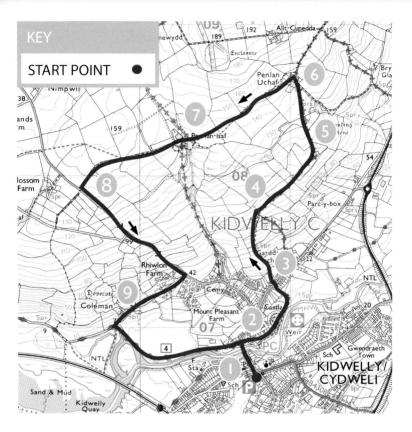

KEY

START POINT ●

steading of Penlan Isaf Farm. Then turn left onto the farm lane and follow it to reach a T-junction with the main road.

8. Turn left onto the road then immediately right to go into a beautiful footpath that is almost totally enclosed by two hedgerows. Walk along this to reach the minor road at the other end and turn left. Head downhill now then go right at the T-junction with the main road. Keep on this to reach a junction just at the start of the 30mph limit then turn right onto Ferry Road, towards Carmarthen Bay Holiday Centre.

9. Keep on this lane to pass Coleman Farm on your right then turn left to go through a metal gap stile onto the Coastal Path. This pleasant, well-surfaced footpath will take you through Glan yr Afon Nature Reserve. Eventually you will arrive at a car park with a ruined building, the old slaughterhouse. From the car park continue to the junction with Bridge Street. Turn right past the Trinity English Methodist Church and retrace your outward journey back to the car park.

ST CLEARS

THIS IS A FASCINATING WALK THROUGH THE VARIED HISTORY OF THIS SMALL TOWN, FROM MEDIEVAL CHURCH AND NORMAN CASTLE TO REBECCA RIOTERS AND THE DISUSED QUAY OF AN ERSTWHILE TRADING TOWN.

The Norman invaders built the castle at St Clears around 1100. It is a classic motte and bailey design, with the defensive motte rising to a height of 25 feet (8m), the highest known in Wales. The castle would have been built in wood and later in stone and if you climb up you will see what a commanding position this would have been. It needed to be since it was attacked and besieged by the Welsh throughout the 12th century. The living quarters for the garrison would have been in the bailey.

The town grew up around the castle and was a thriving centre by the 13th century. The earliest known charter, granted to the town, was in 1392, by Richard II, giving rights to markets and local government. The town hall, opposite the church, was built in 1848, at a cost of £119. The Burgesses of the Corporation were entitled to various privileges, including free dinners and drink, as well as more profitable arrangements, such as access to river crossings and meadows and other resources belonging to the town. It seems that politics has always been a lucrative business.

The Rebecca Riots were similar to uprisings across the country in the 19th century. In the face of grinding poverty and avaricious landlords, the ordinary people were beginning to stir. In this instance, turnpike trusts had established a network of tolls on country roads so that farmers using almost any road to transport goods or beasts had to pay a toll at every turn. The anger at the turnpike trusts grew until a new tollgate at Efailwen in north-west Carmarthenshire was attacked in 1839. The attackers were led by a horseman, disguised as a woman, known as 'Rebecca'. In St Clears, in 1842, when a tollgate was placed near the Mermaid Tavern, making it impossible to pass through the town without paying, 'Rebecca' and her followers demolished it immediately.

The struggle continued as 'Rebecca' and her followers, also dressed in women's clothes, tore down every tollgate that was built. The riots spread and every town had a 'Rebecca', defying the police and the authorities. Eventually a government commission of enquiry reported and the turnpike trusts were reformed in 1844.

THE BASICS

Distance: 2½ miles / 4km

Gradient: Negligible

Severity: Easy

Time: 1½ hrs

Stiles: None

Map: OS Explorer 177 (Carmarthen & Kidwelly)

Path description: Hard paths, woodland path and pavement

Start point: Car park in centre of St Clears (GR SN 280163)

Parking: Car park in centre of St Clears (charges apply) (SA33 4BD)

Landscape: Riverside and town

Dog friendly: Yes

Toilets: At car park

Nearest food: Plenty of places to eat in the town

ST CLEARS WALK

1. From the car park, walk to the river at the far left of the car park and follow the path along the river as it bends under the bridge. Continue along the riverbank passing a wildflower meadow to your right. You will see some waymarkers on the trail with the wild boar emblem of St Clears on them. The church comes into view across the field on your right and the path bends away from the river to a junction of paths.

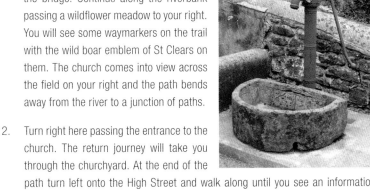

2. Turn right here passing the entrance to the church. The return journey will take you through the churchyard. At the end of the path turn left onto the High Street and walk along until you see an information board and park on the left. This is the site of the Norman motte and bailey castle. Go in and have a walk around the extent of the bailey or courtyard and the motte or mound. In late summer you can collect field mushrooms and blackberries here.

3. Exit the park and turn left to continue along the road. Just before the bridge take the first path to the left leading to the quay. Have a look around the old quay and the information boards and then take the path along the river as far as the bridge, but do not cross the bridge. Take the path to the left, just before the bridge. Pass some gates to your right and follow the narrow path that disappears into the woods.

4. Follow this path to the end. It runs between the ramparts of the bailey on the left and the river on the right. Continue on the path as it becomes tarmac and passes

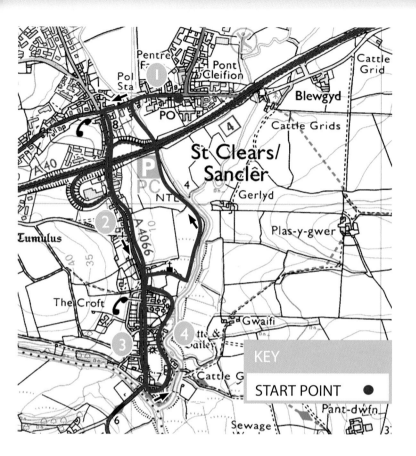

some houses and eventually brings you back to the junction of paths (1) at the church. This time go through the gate into the churchyard and have a look around. Continue to the church and turn right to exit the churchyard on the High Street opposite the town hall.

5. Turn right and continue along the High Street, passing an old water pump on your left and the Butcher's Arms on the right. Further along there is Capel Mair, built in 1862 and then an old school, now a funeral director's. Continue over a bridge over the A40 to a crossroads and turn right into Pentre Road.

6. Go past the car park (1) to find the final points of interest on the town trail. The War Memorial is on the left and a little further along, past the West Wales Centre for Crafts, at the Old Market Square there is a sculpture commemorating the Rebecca Rioters. From here retrace your steps along the street to the car park.

TALLEY

The very strenuous climb on this walk is well rewarded by the panoramic views of the countryside, the village of Talley, its church and ruined abbey.

Talley Abbey was founded here around 1185 under the patronage of Lord Rhys ap Gruffydd. The canons who first came here were from the Premonstratensian Order which had been founded in Prémontré near Laon, France, in 1120 by Saint Norbert. In Britain and Ireland they became known as The White Canons from the colour of their habits. They first arrived in England in 1143 near Lincoln and by the time of the Dissolution of the Monasteries they had 35 houses. Talley is the only one in Wales.

Its remoteness, coupled with a lack of money and continual threats from the nearby Cistercian Order, meant that the grand building originally planned was much reduced in size. When Edward I conquered Wales, the canons were accused of living a dissolute life. The King threatened to clear them out and replace them with English-speaking monks who would lead a religious life. Nevertheless they survived, until they finally fell in 1536 when Henry VIII dissolved all the monasteries.

Locals were quick to cannibalise the stone from the buildings to build houses and barns, but the church survived and remained in use until 1772 when it was in an advanced state of decay and the decision was taken to build a new one nearby. It was built in 1773 with stone taken from the remaining abbey buildings. What now remains of the Abbey was excavated in the 1930s and the outline and what remains of the tower can be visited.

Talley Lakes, which gives the locality its name (Talyllychau, meaning head of lakes) can be seen from the road on the walk uphill. Created in a couple of hollows left by a retreating glacier after the last Ice Age, they served the monks as a fish farm. The remains of a Norman motte can just be made out on the narrow strip that separates the lakes. It's not easy to get close to the lakes and so it attracts a lot of bird life.

They belong to the RSPB and are leased to the Wildlife Trust of South Wales as a nature reserve and there is a hide situated between them. Among the birds that can be seen there are goldeneye, grebes, swans, goosanders and flycatchers.

THE BASICS

Distance: 3¼ miles / 5.2km

Gradient: An exceedingly long uphill section after the first mile

Severity: Strenuous

Time: 2 to 2½ hrs

Stiles: Three

Map: OS Explorer 186 (Llandeilo and Brecha Forest)

Path description: Lane, grass footpaths and forest tracks

Start point: Talley Abbey (GR SN 632327)

Parking: At Talley Abbey (free), just off the B4302 north of Llandeilo (SA19 7AX)

Landscape: Hills, valley, lakes and woodland

Dog friendly: Not very

Toilets: Near the start

Nearest food: In Llandeilo

1. From the car parking area enter the abbey grounds. Exit the grounds and turn right onto the road then immediately turn right again, through a metal gate at a footpath sign to enter the churchyard. The church dates from 1773. It was built with stone from the abbey. Local land-owners, the Williams family of Edwinsford, were responsible for its creation. If you get the chance to have a look inside you will see that it retains its original 18th-century box pews, something of a rarity now. Each one is numbered and would have been allocated to the landowner, his tenants and staff.

2. Leave the churchyard by the main exit and turn right onto a lane. Pass the public toilets and head uphill. To your right you will catch glimpses of the upper and lower Talley lakes. Keep following this lane, passing the house at Penncareg then beyond that, just as the lane is turning right to reach Cilyllyn Fawr, turn left to go through a metal gate by a footpath sign.

3. Head along the right-hand side of this field keeping close to the river. Go over a stile in the top right-hand corner of the field then start to climb up the next one, still keeping to the riverside. The path starts to climb a bit more steeply now to reach a bank where the farmer has put in a wire fence and neglected to include a stile for the right of way. Needless to say a succession of walkers has reduced this to a few inches high and you can easily step over. The going gets a lot tougher now as the gradient increases. You will be climbing for half a mile from the lane to the top. Take it easy and slow, and each time you pause for a breather turn and look back across the valley. Your efforts will be well rewarded by spectacular views. When you cross the next stile bear right and

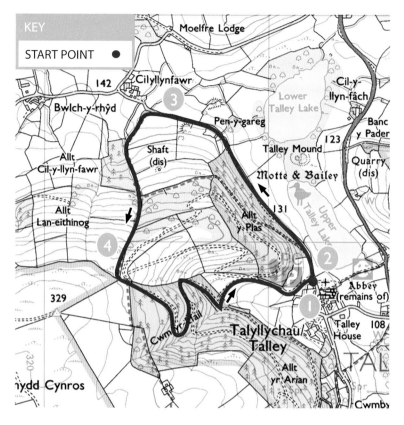

KEY

START POINT ●

follow the path along the fence then round and uphill to finally reach the top by a single waymarker post. To your left is a strategically sited picnic table. This is the best lunch spot in Carmarthenshire with a panoramic view of the area, including the village of Talley below.

4. From here go through a double wooden gate and onto a forest track. Follow this downhill. When you reach a junction with a wooden barrier on your left, keep right on the main track as it twists and turns through the forest on its way downhill. There are occasional inclines but nothing to worry about. At the next junction with a barrier on the left keep right again. Then go through a set of double gates. Bear right where the track splits and the left-hand one heads uphill. Then keep on the track to reach the lane, turn left and return to the start.

RHOSSILI

THIS WALK, ALONG THE CLIFFS OF GOWER, GIVES VIEWS OF
WORMS HEAD BEFORE YOU AND A BEAUTIFUL BAY BELOW
YOU. TURNING INLAND YOU WILL FIND MEDIEVAL STRIP
FIELDS AND A CHARMING 12TH-CENTURY CHURCH.

Gower was the first 'Area of Outstanding Natural Beauty' (AONB), in Britain, with its steep limestone cliffs, eroded into caves, inlets and wide bays. Turn back at Worms Head to look at the sandy bay and, depending on the tide, the surfers riding the white waves to shore. This area has been inhabited from the earliest times, by nomadic hunters of reindeer and mammoth at the end of the Ice Age and by cave dwellers in the Stone Age. In the Bronze and Iron Age, as agriculture developed, the people built defensive hill forts, the remains of which are found all over Gower, including at the start of this walk.

Rarer than hill forts are examples of medieval strip fields. This was a system of allocating land so that each farmer got narrow strips in different parts of the land. In this way, everyone got a fair share of the good land and the more marginal parts. The agricultural revolution, with increasing use of machinery and the development of larger fields concentrated in the ownership of fewer people, destroyed most of these strip systems, which are not practical for modern farming methods. The National Trust has gradually restored the banks and boundaries of these strips.

Don't miss a visit to the little church of St Mary the Virgin. Just inside the door on the left is the ancient 12th-century stone baptismal font. Beside the altar on the right, there is a quaint little window called the Lepers' Window. Previously unglazed, it was said to be the opening through which the lepers received the sacrament. Look too for the stories of Edgar Evans, who died on Scott's expedition to the Antarctic, and William Gibbs, who died in France in the Great War. Finally there is an entertaining story about the rector's wife's complaint about the chimney. The aggrieved architect replied: 'People are very unreasonable about church chimneys.

They will have stoves and warmth but want the chimneys hidden away, the consequence of which is the fires will not draw and the church is filled with smoke …'. When you go back out, have a look at the chimney and see what you think.

THE BASICS

Distance: 2 miles / 3.7km

Gradient: Some gentle slopes

Severity: Easy

Time: 1¼ hrs

Stiles: None

Map: OS Explorer 164 (Gower)

Path description: Grassy paths and stony tracks

Start point: Car park at the Visitor Centre at Rhossili (GR SS 414880)

Parking: Car park at Visitor Centre at Rhossili (not National Trust, so charges apply to everyone, including NT members) (SA3 1PR)

Landscape: Cliffs, beach and fields

Dog friendly: Yes

Toilets: At car park

Nearest food: There are several cafés and pubs in Rhossili

RHOSSILI WALK

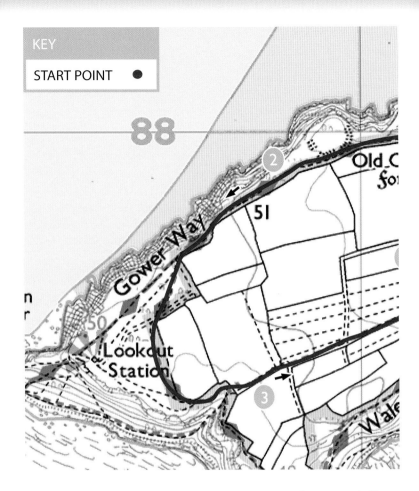

1. From the car park walk down the road past the Visitor Centre towards Worms Head. The road becomes a wide stony track. Continue on this or move onto the grass and follow the track nearer to the cliff (but not too near!) for even more spectacular views. Look out on the right for a series of bumps in the land, which are the faint outline of an Iron Age Fort. When the track turns left continue ahead up a wide grassy bank to the coastguard lookout. Have a good look at Worms Head Island from the cliff top. If the tide is right you can descend the zigzag path to the causeway and walk across. Take note of the warnings displayed. You can only cross here for a couple of hours either side of low tide. It is dangerous to attempt it at any other time.

2. Turn left along the cliff and continue to follow the coast. The views here are

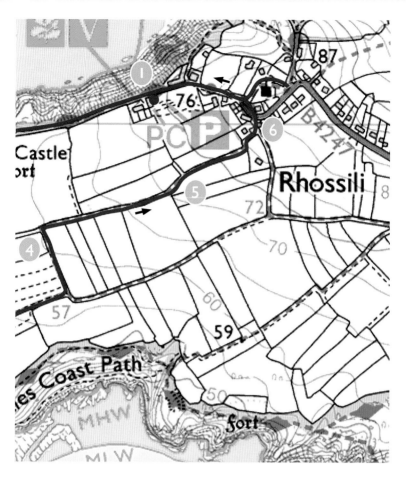

breathtaking. To the right there are glimpses of rocks and beaches and crashing waves at each gully you pass, while look left for an overview of a patchwork of medieval strip fields on the slope. When you come to a gate on the left, you leave the coastal path.

3. Go through the gate and follow a rough track alongside the medieval field network. Have a look at how the boundaries between the strips have

been reinstated. Continue to follow this track through several gates. At the end of the fields turn left across the top of them. Walk to a T-junction and turn right.

4. Continue on this track with hedges of blackberry, hawthorn and fern on either side, ignoring tracks to left or right, and eventually it winds round to a T-junction of tracks at some houses.

5. Turn left here to another T-junction with the road. Turn left again and then shortly right, around the back of a house to some steps up into the churchyard. Have a look around the churchyard and inside the interesting little church. Come out of the church and go left to exit by the other gate.

6. Go left onto the road here and almost immediately left again onto a narrow path around the church. You will come back to the steps again and turn right back to the road. Turn right and return to the car park by the road.

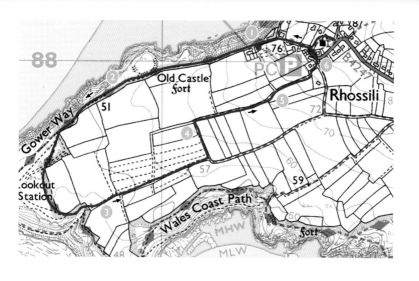

PENMAEN

Neolithic and Norman remains, wonderful sandy beaches and a fairy-tale ruined castle make for an interesting walk.

The most obvious remains on Penmaen Burrows are the earth walls that surrounded a 12th-century Norman castle. As well as the earthen ring work archaeological excavations have uncovered part of a stone-built hall and the Ordnance Survey map shows the location of a Pillow Mound. This was in effect a rabbit warren but not one created by animals. The Normans built them to house the rabbits they brought in for food and for their skins.

Three limestone cliffs that stretch out into the sea give the Three Cliffs Bay its name. The sandy beach of the bay is split in two by Pennard Pill, a large stream that flows towards the sea. It's important that you stick to the walking directions or you won't be able to cross this.

On the top of the Burrows is the majestic ruin of the 12th-century Pennard Castle. It was abandoned in the early 15th century and all that now remains is parts of the curtain wall, tower, gatehouse and hall. In nearby Parkmill the 12th-century mill has fared better, having been renovated and converted to the Gower Heritage Centre, which is home to all manner of craftspeople as well as a museum and tea room.

THE WALK

1.   Exit the car park by turning left, go through a kissing gate then walk to the T-junction at the end of the road. Carefully cross this road then, immediately, turn right and continue down a lane. At a junction bear right and continue, passing the National Trust sign for Notthead, then go downhill on this lane to reach a metal gate leading to a residents' parking area. Pass through a gap to the right of the gate, cross the parking area, then continue down towards the beach on a broad track. When you reach a fingerpost at a junction continue ahead towards Southgate on a narrower path.

2.   At the next junction turn right onto the coastal path which is a narrow path along the edge of the dunes and in summer can be fairly overgrown with ferns but still

THE BASICS

Distance: 5 miles / 8km
Gradient: Fairly flat apart from a couple of climbs. Like the views from the top the climbs will take your breath away, so go slowly
Severity: Strenuous
Time: 3½ hrs
Stiles: None
Map: OS Explorer 164 (Gower)
Path description: Lanes, tracks, sandy footpaths, shingle and beach
Start point: National Trust Car Park at Penmaen (GR SS 531888)
Parking: National Trust car park (free) at Penmaen, just off A4418 (SA3 2HE)
Landscape: Cliffs, coastline, beach and woods
Dog friendly: Yes
Toilets: At the Heritage Centre
Nearest food: Shepherds Store and Cafe or Gower Heritage Centre (both on the walk)

easily followed. Enter a wooded area and follow the waymarkers to keep on the path. Then turn left at the next junction with a fingerpost still following the coast path. The path is now out of the woods and continuing along the edge of the dunes. It is very loose sand so it will slow you down a bit. Cross a small footbridge then come to the National Trust sign for Three Cliffs. There is a fingerpost beside this and you should turn right here and head uphill on a very sandy footpath. It's a bit of a climb to get to the top, so take it slowly. The next set of fingerposts is at the top. Turn left here and follow the coastal path round to reach the entrance to an earthwork fortification with great views. Walk anti-clockwise around the perimeter and then turn right onto a narrow path that heads steeply downhill through woodland. You will need good soles for this as it can be slippy, particularly in wet weather. If you have young children or don't fancy the steep descent then just retrace your steps to the last fingerpost and from there back downhill on the coastal path to the fingerpost at the start of this instruction then turn right. If you continue downhill turn left when you reach a T-junction and walk along a very narrow footpath by the edge of the dune, to exit the wood. This is where the fun starts and older children will love this next bit. The path ends abruptly at a rather steep incline to the right. Turn onto this, lean back and dig in your heels. Then slowly start walking and sliding down. It's very short but very popular.

3. Then turn left along the beach, keeping the dunes on your left. You will work round in a circle to return to the National Trust sign. Retrace your steps from here to the fingerpost then turn right.

4. Now cross the river on a series of stepping blocks. Then follow the direction arrow on the waymarker post and bear left along the shingle beach to a waymarker post ahead. Ignore this and turn left heading along a sandy path.

5. When this splits, bear right onto the path heading uphill. Again this is loose sand and will slow you down but it is not as steep as the previous incline. There are many paths splitting off from this; they all go to the same place: the castle. The going gets easier when you reach some steps and afterwards find duckboarding just under the sand providing a bit more traction. Eventually reach the castle and reap the rewards of your labours by enjoying the most spectacular views. Then pass through the Castle Arch and continue along the footpath. Look out for a post with a blank white waymarker on it to your left and take this path, following other white markers and then a series of white stones that indicate the line of the path across the golf course. This passes just in front of the 6th tee then, after another white stone, turns left to reach a marker post with various options. Keep ahead on a broad sandy path to cross just in front of the next tee then veer right onto a well-surfaced footpath. This soon enters woodland and the condition deteriorates. Keep on the main path as it twists and turns downhill through the woods. At a fingerpost

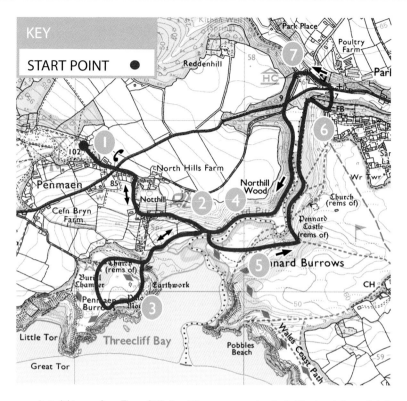

turn right away from Three Cliffs Bay. When you come to a footbridge turn left over it, left again at the end of the path that reaches the road, then cross the road and treat yourself at Shepherd's Store and Coffee Shop.

6. Turn right out of Shepherd's and follow this minor road to reach the Gower Heritage Centre, cross the ford, or take the bridge over the river then turn left and follow the road to a T-junction.

7. Turn right onto the road then cross over and turn immediately left onto a footpath signed for Penmaen and Three Cliffs Bay. At the next junction turn left following the sign in the direction of Three Cliffs Bay. This path is rather muddy and initially goes through woodland. Then it emerges to continue alongside a river with views of the castle above you to the left. Eventually you will reach the stepping blocks you crossed on the outward Directions. Turn right here and follow the outward route back to Penmaen.

PORT EYNON

THIS IS AN EXHILARATING WALK ALONG THE CLIFFS ABOVE DRAMATIC WAVES CRASHING ONTO THE ROCKS. A SHORT DETOUR TAKES YOU TO A SECRET SMUGGLERS' HOLE.

At the start of the walk you pass the Youth Hostel, which was built as a lifeboat station in 1884. Towards the end of the walk, at the churchyard, look for the memorial to coxswain William Gibbs and lifeboat crew William Eynon and George Harry, who were all lost at sea while trying to rescue the steamship Dunvegan in 1916.

Smuggling was rife in this area as in many coastal towns in the 17th, 18th and 19th centuries, partly due to the heavy duties on goods such as brandy, tobacco and tea. The 16th-century Salt House, which you pass near the start of the walk, was the home of the Lucas family, one of the most notorious smuggling families in the area. It was said to have secret tunnels leading to smuggling caves, but no evidence has been found to support that idea. However, given the value of salt and contraband, it was probably well defended against both thieves and authorities.

The Culver Hole is also supposed to have secret tunnels leading away from it. It is a natural fissure in the rocks that has been walled in with doors and windows. It was used as a pigeon loft, which provided a source of food and enabled the smugglers to send messages by pigeon post. It was also used to store contraband, and if you manage to get down to it, you will realise what a perfect hiding place it would have been. You could walk to within a few yards of it and turn back without seeing it, tucked into the cliff.

Stories abound of the struggle between the smugglers and the revenue men. It could be a dangerous business and men on both sides of the law were shot dead in the skirmishes. Contraband would be hidden by villagers everywhere, even in the church. One story tells of a barrel of brandy that the revenue men had discovered in the loft of a barn.

They decided to lie in wait for the smugglers' return. However, the locals held a party in the barn with much revelling and gaiety, and when it was over the customs men discovered that the barrel had been drilled and emptied before their very eyes.

THE BASICS

Distance: 3 miles / 4.8km

Gradient: One very steep climb

Severity: Moderate

Time: 2 hrs

Stiles: None

Map: OS Explorer 164 (Gower)

Path description: Dirt, grassy and stony paths and road

Start point: Car park at Port Eynon (GR SS 467851)

Parking: Car park at Port Eynon, at end of A4118 (SA3 1NN)

Landscape: Coast, cliffs and road

Dog friendly: Yes

Toilets: At the car park

Nearest food: Plenty of places to eat in Port Eynon

PORT EYNON WALK

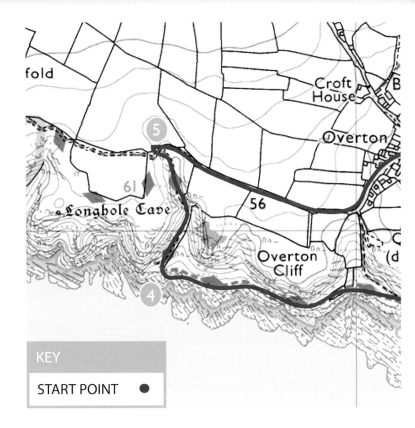

KEY

START POINT ●

1. From the car park head past the roundabout towards the beach and turn right along the coastal path to the Youth Hostel. This is an old lifeboat station. Turn right here up some steps and follow the path to a junction at a caravan park. Turn left here along a permissive path through the camp site and exit at a gate on the left.

2. Pass the remains of the Salt House on the left and bear right up a steep stony path to the cliff top. In front of you, you will see the monument to Gwent Jones and Stephen Lee, founder members of the Gower Society. Turn right here and look for a tiny unmarked path leading down to the left towards the sea. If weather and tide allow, go down here right to the bottom and you will see Culver's Hole tucked into the cliff face. Return to the coastal path and turn left.

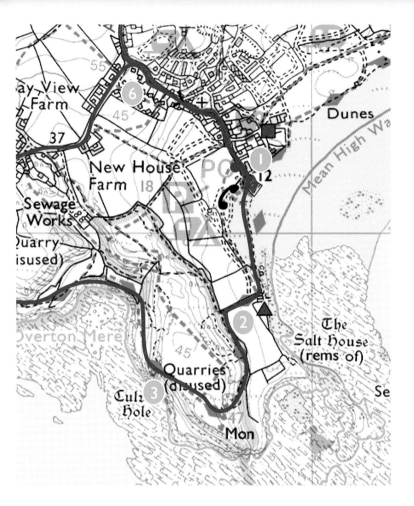

3. Follow coastal path waymarkers descending through an area of gorse and through a gate and along the path above the beach. Where the path forks, bear left. Go through a gate marked Overton Cliff Wildlife Trust. At this point the sea crashes wildly into the rocks of the bay to the left while the cliff rises starkly to the right. Eventually go through another gate labelled Long Hole Cliff.

4. Head up the grassy path with a wall on the

right and cliffs on either side ahead. At the top of the path at a T-junction of paths turn right.

5. Go along this path, through a gate and then on to a gate onto the road. Go down the road and through the village of Overton. Turn right at a junction and continue to the next junction and turn right again.

6. Go down the road to the church, stop to have a look at the memorial to the lifeboat men and then turn right down into Port Eynon. From the roundabout retrace your steps to the car park.

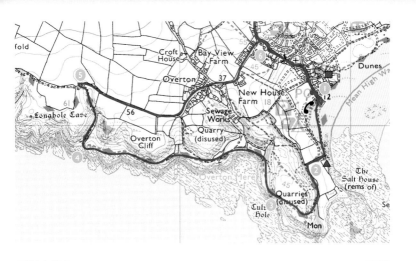

CARMARTHEN

Enjoy this gentle stroll round the oldest town in Wales, passing various historical remains that will help to tell you its story.

The Romans arrived in this part of Wales around 73–74 CE. They constructed a series of roads to link their Tywi Valley forts at Llandovery, Llandeilo and Carmarthen, built to subjugate and control the indigenous Demetae tribe. There are still a few remains of the Roman occupation that you will visit on this walk. Although Carmarthen started life as a military fort it had become a walled town by the 3rd century. It is now the oldest continually occupied town in Wales. Although only a fragment of the Roman architecture can be seen, the line of the original walls can still be followed in the patterns of the street and there is no doubt that underneath the current town there are lots of unexcavated Roman remains.

Carmarthen Castle was built in 1106–9 by Henry I in his continual quest to control the Welsh Princes. Originally a motte and bailey construction, the present structure replaced it in the 13th century. Famously it was captured and held briefly by the legendary Owen Glyndŵr in the early 15th century. It last saw action during the English Civil War from 1642 to 1645.

Just in front of the castle is Nott Square, which was the town's first market in 1240. Fragments of the Market Cross that stood here until 1783 can be seen in the museum. The covered market that continued on this spot was pulled down in the mid-19th century to make way for the statue of the town's most famous soldier, General Nott. In front of this you will see a plaque commemorating the Protestant Bishop Dr Robert Ferrar, who was burned at the stake here in 1555.

THE WALK

1.   Exit the car park by walking towards Wilko's supermarket then passing it on the right-hand side. Go through an exit that has two posts, to prevent traffic using it, and then turn left. Continue along Greyfriars Street behind the supermarket. Pass the colourfully decorated building of Carmarthen Youth Project and go onto a paved footpath running alongside a metal fence. To your left, behind the fence and on the other side of the path you can see all that remains of the Civil War fortifications. Continue from here to go down some steps, then turn left then right to cross the road, then left again on the other side.

THE BASICS

Distance: 3½ miles / 5.6km

Gradient: Mostly flat

Severity: Easy

Time: 2½ to 3 hrs

Stiles: None

Map: OS Explorer 177 (Carmarthen & Kidwelly)

Path description: Mostly pavement. A couple of short sections on footpaths

Start point: Merlin's Walk, Carmarthen (GR SN 410199)

Parking: Merlin's Walk shopping cenrre, Carmarthen (SA31 3BN)

Landscape: Townscape and streets

Dog friendly: Yes

Toilets: At bus station under the car park And in Carmarthen Park on the walk

Nearest food: Lots of eating places in Merlin's Walk and Lammas Street

2. Turn right through a gate and up some steps to reach Carmarthen Park. This has been here since 1900 and has the oldest, surviving, concrete velodrome, still in use, in the UK. Walk round the park past the bandstand, the stone circle, an outdoor gym and a rather splendid tea house, to exit via a set of iron gates, then cross the street and turn left.

3. Turn right into Lammas Street, passing the late 19th-century Christ Church, on the right, the Gothic English Congregational Church, with its distinctive spire, on the left, and the early 18th-century Lammas Street Chapel on the right. Almost immediately on your left now in the centre of the street is the memorial to the men of the Royal Welch Fusiliers who died during the Crimean War. Further along Lammas Street, on the right is the Boar's Head Hotel, one of the oldest coaching inns in Wales.

4. Turn left into Mansell Street. Follow it to pass the Mansell Arms on your left then keep ahead, across a square to pass the indoor market and the clock tower before turning right in the direction of King Street. Keep ahead, past Marks and Spencer, along Merlane Lane towards the Coracle Tavern then turn right again. Proceed to the end of this street then , as the road turns left, keep ahead along a pathway and through a garden then bear left to go up a narrow lane then turn left into King Street.

5. Stroll along here passing the old Post Office building on your right, then the offices of the Carmarthen Journal, the oldest newspaper in Wales. Near the top of the street have a look at the library on your left. This was Furnace House built in 1760 for a local ironmaster, Robert Morgan. Opposite it stands St Peter's Church, which has been there from at least the 12th century, making it the oldest building in the town. Turn right down Church Lane.

6. Now turn left into Church Street. Follow it to Priory Street and walk along this for a considerable distance passing a roundabout, then on the right, a war memorial, St John's Church and then another roundabout. Cross the road here to visit the site of The Old Oak. Merlin the Magician was allegedly born in this town and his birthplace was nearby. The Oak was associated with his prophecy that ' When

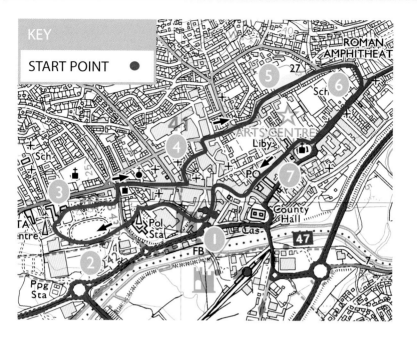

Priory's Oak will tumble down, Then shall fall Carmarthen Town. It was long dead by the mid 19th century and despite objections was removed in 1978 to improve the traffic flow. The town survived. Just along Priory Street from here on your left is the excavated remains of the Roman Amphitheatre, one of only four that existed in Wales. Now retrace your steps back along Priory Street, turn left to go down Old Priory Road, through an arch and follow the lane round to the left. At the bottom an interpretation board will explain that this was once the site of the Medieval Priory of St John.

7.   Continue down the lane, turn right then, as the lane rises, bear left through a gate and along a footpath. When it reaches a car park keep to the right-hand edge to exit it then turn right up the side of The Warehouse, follow the road up left then right then turn left into Spillman Street. Continue to the end then cross over and enter the grounds of the County Hall. Keep right to enter the Castle then pass the tourist office and exit the castle grounds via the main gate into Nott Square. Head past the statue and down Hall Street to go through Guildhall then to Dark Gate and turn right into Lammas Street. Turn left into Merlin's Walk shopping centre passing the huge wooden carving of the wizard to re-enter the car park.

SWANSEA

Explore Dylan Thomas's 'ugly lovely town', much changed since his day, around the renovated dockside area and marina, but closer to his experience as you pass his birthplace and his favourite boyhood haunt, Cymdonkin Park.

There are other walks in this book with connections to Dylan Thomas but this one will take you back to the very beginning of his short but fascinating life story. He was born in the front bedroom of number 5 Cwmdonkin Drive on 27 October 1914 and this small, semi-detached house and the town of his birth were to have a huge influence on shaping his life and his writing. It was his home for the first 19 years of his life. He started writing poetry in his cramped bedroom in his late teens, producing over 200 poems in four notebooks. Over half of his final published output was written at the tiny desk there.

Not far from the house is Cwmdonkin Park. It was created in 1874 and, although small, was one of Dylan's favourite boyhood haunts. It was created by landscaping the grounds round an old reservoir, which had earlier been filled in with rubble.

Thomas was first taken there as a baby in a pram and throughout his childhood it featured heavily in his life as a place to play and let his imagination run free. Unsurprisingly it features in his poetry and radio broadcasts. His poem, 'The Hunchback in the Park', from his 1930–32 notebook, is about Mr Smallcombe, the council park-keeper, whom the children called 'Old Smalley'. They tormented him mercilessly and goaded him to the point that he would throw the pointed stick, that he used to spear litter, at them, hitting Thomas on the leg on one occasion.

There's a memorial garden to the poet in the park. In it there is a memorial stone inscribed with the last three lines from the poem 'Fern Hill'. This had been inspired by his childhood visits to the farm of his aunt and uncle near Llangain.

Other memorials to the poet in Swansea include the Dylan Thomas Theatre. Its waterside base was built 35 years ago and it is the home of the Swansea Little Theatre, a group that Thomas and his sister both joined; they appeared in several of their productions. There's a bronze statue of Thomas in the square in front of the theatre.

THE BASICS

Distance: 5 miles / 8km

Gradient: Mainly flat, a few gentle slopes

Severity: Easy

Time: 3 hrs

Stiles: None

Map: OS Explorer 165 (Swansea)

Path description: Pavement, quayside, park

Start point: Swansea railway station (GR SS 657936)

Parking: At the station or nearby town centre car park (station postcode SA1 1NU)

Landscape: Town, quay and park

Dog friendly: Not ideal

Toilets: At the station

Nearest food: There are many restaurants, pubs and cafés in Swansea

SWANSEA WALK

1. From the station, head to the High Street and go along as far as the castle and turn right into Castle Square and immediately left into Princess Way. Bear left on Princess Way into York Street to reach a main road. Cross the road to Cambrian Way and the Swansea Museum. This is an old-fashioned museum with a little bit of everything, including an Egyptian mummy, so it's well worth pausing here to investigate.

2. Leave the Museum and turn right and then left into Adelaide Road. At the end, turn right into Somerset Place, where you will see the Dylan Thomas Centre on your left. Turn right here into East Burrows Road and go along as far as Pockets Wharf and turn right into Manheim Quay. You now have the Tawe Basin to your left and the strange little Mannheim Water Tower ahead of you. When you reach this, continue along the quay with the Pump House ahead of you and the Marina to your left. Pass to the right of the Pump House and you will see the Dylan Thomas Theatre to your right and in the square beyond a statue of Dylan Thomas.

3. Continue along Victoria Quay with the National Waterfront Museum to your right and renovated historic boats in the basin to your left. At the end of the quay turn left towards a tall white tower building, which dominates the view. Continue to a road and cross over and ascend some steps, with ramps for wheelchairs. Go down on the other side to the promenade and turn right along it. Continue along the promenade or on the sands until you reach an old partially dismantled footbridge. Cross the road here and turn left.

4. Shortly turn right into Gorse Lane. Go up Gorse Lane and then straight across at a junction into Finsbury Terrace. At the top of Finsbury Terrace, turn right into Marlborough Road and then left into Rhyddings Park Road and on into Gwdyr Crescent. Gwdyr Crescent winds round into Gwdyr Square.

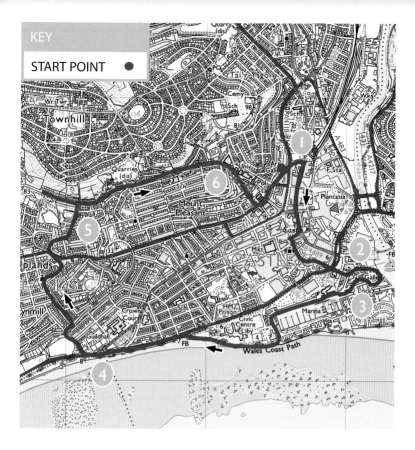

KEY

START POINT ●

5. At the traffic lights here go right and immediately left into Uplands Terrace. At the top go right into Cwmdonkin Close and then immediately left into Cwmdonkin Drive. Dylan Thomas's birthplace is at number 5. It is privately owned but has been restored to be as it might have been in Dylan Thomas's time and house tours are available. From the house go on to the top of the road and turn left to go to Cwmdonkin Park. This is a lovely park and one where Dylan Thomas spent many hours as a boy. This is an ideal place for a picnic. Leave the park and return to the junction with Cwmdonkin Road. Go straight ahead on Penlan Terrace and then onto Terrace Road, which continues after a pedestrian barrier, eventually reaching Mount Pleasant to the right.

6. Wind down Mount Pleasant to traffic lights opposite a university building. Turn left into Alexandra Road and return to the station.

MARGAM

INDULGE IN A SPOT OF TIME TRAVEL AND CATCH UP WITH THE EXPLOITS OF CAPTAIN JACK HARKNESS, THE TORCHWOOD TEAM FROM THE BBC SCI-FI SERIES, AND DOCTOR WHO.

Margam Country Park was once the home of the wealthy Mansel Talbot family but its history is much older than that. About 3,000 years ago Bronze Age people farmed on Margam mountain. Much later, during the Iron Age, the Silures tribe inhabited this part of Wales and there are the remains of two hilltop settlements you can visit.

Celtic crosses found in the area suggest that Margam may have been a centre of the Celtic Church but the earliest religious building in the park is the Cistercian abbey, founded in 1147 by the Earl of Gloucester. The Cistercians' wealth, founded on raising sheep and producing wool, made it the wealthiest monastery in Wales at one time.

Following the Dissolution of the Monasteries the land was acquired by Sir Rice Mansel, who altered the monastic buildings to create accommodation. Over the centuries the estate was enhanced first by the construction of a Tudor mansion, then gardens were added and by the late 18th century the Orangery was built. By 1830 the construction of Margam Castle had begun and the surrounding land had been made into a series of parks.

Christopher Mansel Talbot, who built Margam Castle, was a Member of Parliament and introduced a bill in 1834 to improve the harbour at Aberavon and later, another to extend it. It was later renamed Port Talbot. He was also involved in the South Wales Railway Company and invested in the Port Talbot Ironworks.

The estate remained in the Mansel Talbot family until it was sold to a brewer in 1942. During the war years it was requisitioned by the government and housed troops.

Abandoned and derelict, it was eventually purchased by Glamorgan County Council in 1973, but then extensively damaged by fire in 1977. Since then a long and careful restoration process has brought it back to life.

THE BASICS

Distance: 5 miles/ 8km

Gradient: A climb up to the Pulpit but otherwise flat

Severity: Easy to moderate

Time: 2½ to 3½ hrs but aim to spend a day in the park if you can

Stiles: None.

Map: OS Explorer 165 (Swansea)

Path description: Estate roads, tracks, well-surfaced footpaths, rough tracks and footpaths and grass tracks

Start point: Car park at Margam Country Park (GR SS 801860)

Parking: Margam Country Park (charges apply) (SA13 2TJ)

Landscape: Parkland, river, hills, woodland and coastline

Dog friendly: Very

Toilets: Several in the park: near the entrance, at the visitor centre and at the Orangery

Nearest food: Visitor centre at the castle

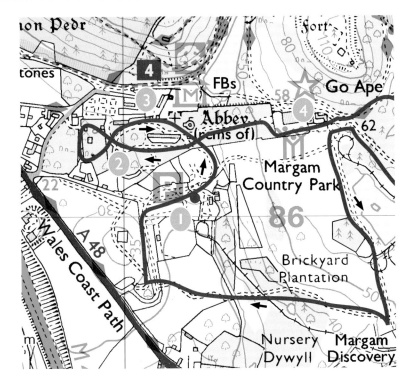

1. Exit the car park and enter the park via the entrance kiosk where you need to pay the parking fee. The park itself is free. Then follow the path as it curves to the left to go through an opening in the wall and head towards the ruins of the abbey. Then turn left, head along the path to reach the front of the Orangery. Fans of Torchwood will recognise this as the venue for the wedding of Rhys and Gwen in one episode.

2. Keep to the path as it curves to the right to reach the entrance to Fairytale Land. Go inside but be warned: if you have small children you will have the greatest of difficulties persuading them to come back out!

3. Leave the village when you can and keep ahead on a footpath to pass the toilets. Then turn right at the end of the first greenhouse to go through an alley and turn right again to enter the Citrus House. When you have finished there retrace your steps and continue along the path past the toilets. Turn left into the gardens on your right then turn right and work your way up through several ornamental gardens. When you can go no further turn right through a gap in the hedge then left back onto the footpath and almost immediately right again through a gate. Then turn left onto another footpath that runs along behind the Orangery to reach the Abbey Church. Continue past the

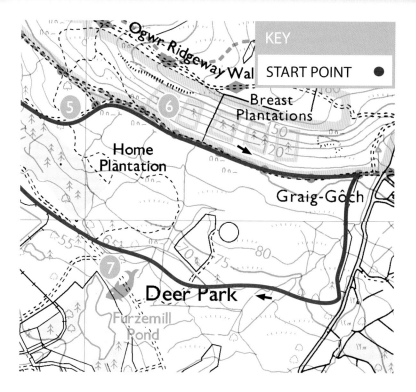

abbey ruins making towards the castle. Climb the steps to the castle, turn right then left at the end of the gardens and walk along towards the café and visitor centre.

4.   Walk past the blue Police Box, which is actually Doctor Who's Tardis. Regular followers of the time-travelling Doctor may have feelings of déjà vu. Hardly suprising, as Margam has been used several times as a location.

5.   Go along the path ahead to reach a waymarker post in front of double deer gates. Follow the blue route, through the gates and on up the track keeping right at the first junction.

6.   At the next junction turn right then bear left, uphill on a track still following the blue markers. You now have a long, slow, but gentle climb. Once you get to the top it levels off and you can continue over flat ground to reach the Pulpit Stone. The views from here are magnificent. When you have rested continue along the track to reach a waymarker post. Bear right here across open ground in the direction indicated by the arrow. The grassy path goes through a gap in the bracken and then bears right again, heading downhill. Soon the grassy track becomes more distinct, then rutted,

then rocky, all the time descending. Follow it as it twists and turns downhill then at a junction bear right following the blue marker. At the next junction leave the blue route and follow the Family Bike Trail, straight ahead. You are now on a well-surfaced track. Bear left at the next junction and right at the one after that. This will return to a T-junction with your outward route where you should turn left and head downhill to go through the deer gate and back to the Castle Visitor Centre.

7.   Now take a left turn onto an estate road just beyond the train terminus. Follow it past a lake on your left, an adventure playground on your right then keep ahead, past the Farm Trail to reach the Discovery Centre. Retrace your steps from here then turn left into the Farm Trail. Don't forget to use the gel to disinfect your hands if you have been petting the animals. Then turn left onto a footpath that eventually leads back to the car park.

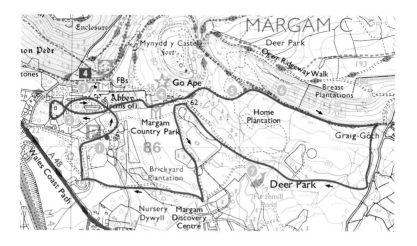

8. But first it runs through the Wood Vibrations Trail that goes past a series of giant wooden musical instruments created with the help of local children. Then go through two gates, take a sharp left turn and continue on the path by the river to cross a bridge. Then follow the long, narrow footpath, past toilets and finally turn left to re-enter the car park.

GNOLL

THE ONCE MAGNIFICENT GEORGIAN COUNTY HOUSE
HAS NOW BEEN RAZED TO THE GROUND, BUT YOU CAN
APPRECIATE THE GROUNDS AND THE PONDS. THEN TAKE OFF
THROUGH THE WOODS FOR A TRANQUIL WALK.

The rich merchant Evans family bought the estate in 1658 and built a house, which gradually over several generations became a mansion. The estate passed to the Mackworth family through the marriage of Mary Evans to Sir Humphrey Mackworth in 1686. He built mills and furnaces, which produced iron and brass and made the family even richer. Much of the extension and beautification of the estate and house followed in the early 18th century. Formal gardens were created, the house was extended and the cascades were made through Fishpond Wood and Mosshouse Woods. By the late 18th century grand north and south wings had been added to the house as well as a series of follies, such as the grotto and the Ivy Tower.

In 1811 the estate was bought by the Grant family and remained in their hands for most of the century, but gradually diminishing as they sold parts of the estate and demolished parts of the house. The estate was eventually taken over in 1923 by Neath Borough Council and the house continued to deteriorate until it was demolished in 1957. The estate too was neglected until the restoration began in 1984.

The restoration has turned a sad and neglected estate into a beautiful parkland with activities for all ages. The cascades, which had become overgrown, have been restored to their original glory and paths have been laid out throughout the estate for walking. Investigate the arboretum planted around the house by the Mackworth family in the 18th century, which now has mature specimens of oak, lime, sweet chestnut and giant redwood among others. Don't miss the Hollow Oak near the Visitors' Centre. Children will love climbing right into the middle of it. It has been in this condition for over 60 years and is still thriving.

Gnoll is home to a great diversity of wildlife. The ponds support fish, insects, frogs, newts and toads as well as ducks, swans and geese. Daubenton's and noctule bats – the latter one of the largest species of bat in the UK – thrive in the woods next to the fishpond, where they can be seen in the early evening swooping over the pond for insects.

THE BASICS

Distance: 2 miles / 3.2km
Gradient: Some gentle slopes
Severity: Easy
Time: 1½ to 2 hrs
Stiles: None
Map: OS Explorer 165 (Swansea)
Path description: Tarmac, stony and woodland paths
Start point: Car park at Gnoll Estate Country Park (GR SS 765975)
Parking: Gnoll Estate Country Park, just east of Neath (SA11 3BS)
Landscape: Country estate, woodland
Dog friendly: Yes
Toilets: At the Visitor Centre
Nearest food: At the Visitor Centre

GNOLL WALK

1. From the car park walk towards the fishpond and go right to the Visitor Centre. Pass the centre and go on along the pond to the end. At some signposts turn right away from the pond, following the signpost for the Gnoll House cellars. Look out on your left for the ha-ha (or recessed wall), which is at the end of the terrace from the house.

2. The path bends gently left towards the site of the house. Look for a right fork, which leads to the ice house. Turn and then go down some steps to investigate it. Ice was brought here from the Arctic in summer and from closer to home in winter. Return to the path and continue to the outline of the house. Look for the entrance to the cellars, down some steps to a door. This is where the wine collection was stored. Then head across to the steps up to the viewing point to have an overview of the house shape. When you exit the viewing platform, turn right onto a path through the woods. This descends to some steps and re-joins the main track. Follow it round, by a wall and through some gates to the path, which leads back to the pond. At the pond go right across the top of the pond to the other side.

3. Turn left to follow the edge of the pond to a wooden bridge and the French Cascades. Turn right and go up alongside the cascades to the top. At the top turn left and then immediately right over a bridge and continue up the path beside the stream. At the top turn left and head down the track.

4. Look out on the right for a path leading down to a bridge over the stream. Turn right over another bridge and go straight ahead. Continue on this stony path, passing an area of clear felled forest; you can see the Guinea Pond below you to the left. This was clear felled because of an outbreak of the tree disease Phytophthora ramorum. Continue to the end of the clear felled area and then turn left.

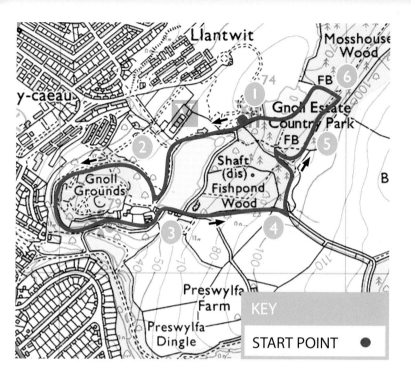

5. Go down by the clear felled area and turn left onto a path, which eventually meanders back through forest. Look out on the right for where the path crosses the stream. You need to jump across, but it is only about a foot. The woodland path emerges onto a wider path. Turn right and continue along the Guinea Pond.

6. At the end of the pond turn right across a bridge and follow the edge of the pond to the end. Turn right down a grassy bank to join the road back to the car park.

ABOUT THE AUTHORS

Moira McCrossan and Hugh Taylor are a husband and wife writing team now specialising in travel for the over 50's and walking guides. They are also travel editors of the UK's premier over 50's web site laterlife.com.

Moira McCrossan spent most of her working life in education and was a Primary School Head Teacher. An active trade unionist she is a former President of the Educational Institute of Scotland, served on the general council of the Scottish TUC and the executive committee of the Women's National Commission for whom she co-authored the report, Growing up Female in the UK. She was also a frequent contributor to the Times Educational Supplement (Scotland).

Hugh Taylor is an Award winning travel writer, broadcaster and photographer. He worked extensively for BBC Radio, producing several series for Radio 2 including Doomsday in the Afternoon about the music of the Scottish Travellers.

Together they have written or contributed to over forty travel and outdoor guides, some of which have been translated into several languages. They range from major country guides covering Scotland, Lebanon and Jordan to walking books throughout the UK. Their work has appeared worldwide in publications as diverse as The Times, Women's Realm, Choice, The Herald, Interval World and the Glencairn Gazette. They live in the picturesque southern Scottish village of Moniaive and in Capena, a hill town just north of Rome.

The Authors would like to thank the team at the Camping and Caravanning Club Press Office for all their help.